From Phansi Yard

From Phansi Yard

My Year with the Women
of Yerawada

Sudha Bharadwaj

JUGGERNAUT BOOKS
C-I-128, First Floor, Sangam Vihar, Near Holi Chowk,
New Delhi 110080, India

First published by Juggernaut Books 2023

10 9 8 7 6 5 4 3 2 1

P-ISBN: 9789353451868
E-ISBN: 9789353451844

Typeset in Adobe Caslon Pro by R. Ajith Kumar, Noida

Printed at Thomson Press India Ltd

To all the unjustly incarcerated
And for Maaysha, who suffered my absence the most

Contents

Introduction

An early morning knock on my door took me into a world of incarceration, first at home and then in prison, where I wrote the sketches of women prisoners and comments on jail life that comprise this book. Who was I up to that moment and how had I lived my life? The editorial team at Juggernaut Books felt readers would want to know. But when I sat down to compress six decades into a chapter, I thought how much easier this would be if they just asked me some questions. They did, and here are my responses.

Your life comes across as a series of unusual choices, the path less travelled, as you've put it. For example, you gave up American citizenship at twenty-one. How did you come to acquire it, and why did you relinquish it instead of packing your bags for America like so many other IIT graduates?

I was born on 1 November 1961 in Boston in the United States (US), where my parents, Krishna and Ranganath Bharadwaj, were both postdoctoral fellows in economics. I was probably an unplanned baby as my parents were on a shoestring budget.

That's how I got American citizenship – by birth. We returned to India when I was about one, so I have no memories of America. But photographs of me as an infant show me being babysat by our neighbours – an immigrant Russian couple and their son Gregory. Apparently, I was angelic with them, sleeping throughout the day, only to keep my tired parents up all night. The photos show a thin Krishna Bharadwaj cradling me. She has dark circles under her eyes but is nevertheless radiant in her motherhood.

My mother told me that Professor P.C. Mahalanobis, then associated with the Planning Commission, had come to talk to bright young Indian economists in the US encouraging them to join in the nation-building effort. My mother was one of those who responded with enthusiasm.

So your parents returned to India?

They came back to work in India. But they effectively separated when I was around four, even if their formal divorce came much later. Though I remember some joyous indulgences with my father, I was terrified by the loud, raised voices when my parents argued. I remember locking myself in a bathroom and having to be cajoled to come out, and hugging my mother's knees and pleading during an ugly fight: 'Oh, why don't you just accept whatever he is saying!' According to my mother that was when she decided she needed to part ways with my father. She accepted the opportunity of a fellowship in Cambridge, which came on the invitation of Piero Sraffa – a brilliant Marxian economist and close associate of Antonio Gramsci. Professor Sraffa had been deeply impressed by an excellent review my mother had published of his cryptic classic, *Production of Commodities by Means of Commodities*. For me, this meant a childhood in the university town of Cambridge, in the United Kingdom, and primary schooling at the Newnham Croft County Primary School there. There were some hard days too. My mother was diagnosed with TB and my grandmother had to come to live with us – a non-English-speaking nine-yard-sari-wearing conservative Brahmin lady, shivering in the Cambridge winters – but one who nevertheless loved her rebellious daughter.

You were a three-woman family. How did that work?

I think my grandmother suppressed my spontaneity and made me very dutiful and obedient, and a bit cowardly too: 'Don't be a trouble to your mother!' – something that I still resent in my character. But from the hindsight of an adult, I have to admit she rescued us. I made my first very good friend – Jinny, Tanjam Narasimhan – who got back in touch recently after half a century. Jinny's mother Sita was also a single mother and a professor of English literature. We lived a lot in each other's houses. I have a distinct memory as a child of helping my mother proofread one of her most famous works, *Production Conditions in Indian Agriculture*, sitting with copies fanned out in front of me and marking in the corrections as she read them out. My mother never had any intention of settling abroad, so when racism started rearing its ugly head even in a liberal university town like Cambridge, with our key disappearing from under the doormat one day, or my getting threatening phone calls with sexual innuendoes when I was home alone, she made the move back to Delhi. I was ten or eleven when we came back, after six years in England.

Was your mother a role model?

My mother was the most important influence in my life before I met the trade union leader Shankar Guha Niyogi, though like all daughters of an awe-inspiring mother, I resented being in her shadow. She was not just a brilliant economist but a gifted singer of Hindustani classical music. Her values of simplicity and sincerity, respect towards colleagues and subordinates alike, love of students and teaching, I think I imbibed by sheer osmosis. She was an undeclared socialist since her childhood. Her home town Karwar, in Karnataka, was deeply influenced by the socialists who were organizing Goa's liberation movement from across the border. In 1972, she set up the Centre for Economic Studies and Planning at Jawaharlal Nehru University (JNU) with other brilliant heterodox economists like Professor Sunanda Sen, Professors Prabhat and Utsa Patnaik, Professor Amit Bhaduri, etc. This Centre, with its unique curriculum, was eventually to produce the most insightful and critical work on the economic development of India, and she poured a lot of energy into it. I used to joke that the Centre was more her baby than I was. It was not easy being the only child of a very busy woman; I might have occasionally felt bad about her not being there to open the door when I came home from school. But she certainly expanded my horizon of what a woman could be, and with grace and confidence.

You spent your formative years living on university campuses. Did you like that life?

I have idyllic memories of my Cambridge childhood – of my mother punting down the river Cam in her sari, feeding the ducks by the river, our free school lunches and milk (since Thatcherite cuts had not yet kicked in), and many Indian students dropping in for vegetarian meals and advice. I loved the children's section of the city library where my mother would drop me when she was busy, and the friendly librarian too, and that's where I developed my love for reading.

My schooldays were spent in the JNU campus, and I studied at the Central School in the IIT Delhi campus close by. In those days, children of professors and karmacharis (workers) studied together in the school and we went to school in Delhi Transport Corporation buses. It meant that we were never cocooned, as upper-middle-class kids are today. The JNU campus was a really lovely place to grow up in as a child. It was an undulating terrain with lots of trees and Nalanda-like brick buildings. It had the scope for long walks and was extremely safe, with young girls and boys moving around till late at night. There were many cultural events and discussions around current topics in the hostel messes and on the lawns. Elections were neither a show of muscle nor of money power but rather a time of heated discussions on esoteric political topics, like 'Is Albania really communist?' I recall as a teenager seeing faculty and students gathering on the lawns in front of our house to sing '*Surya ast ho gaya, gagan mast ho gaya*' (The sun has set and the sky is afire with joy), a popular song of the pre-Independence Indian National Army, on the occasion of Vietnam's liberation. I also remember the triumphant early morning procession of students celebrating the defeat of Sanjay Gandhi and Indira Gandhi in the 1977 elections. The atmosphere both in the campus and in my house was that we had to work hard to change our country for the better.

Why a five-year maths degree at IIT Kanpur? What did you plan to do with it?

I was a pretty good student at school and loved history, literature and mathematics. Charles Dickens was my favourite writer in childhood, and when we returned to India the transition to learning Hindi was made easier not only by my fortunately quick grasp of languages but even more by my falling equally in love with Premchand. The history of the freedom struggle was a passion with me since school, and still is. Mathematics I was good at, though interestingly, not at arithmetic; it was more the logic, patterns and abstraction that I would find beautiful and fascinating. Given a choice I would have studied all three, but in those days no school could have possibly permitted such a crazy combination of subjects. So like all bright students, I got pushed towards the science stream and therefore mathematics.

Two of my best friends at Central School – Damanjeet and Bandana – were giving entrance examinations for the medical and engineering streams and joined coaching classes to do so. It was more a peer group thing for me to join too, and so I attempted the IIT Joint Entrance Examination and was lucky. That year the maths exam was pretty tough and I hear that the marks in maths became the threshold for admission, so my definitely poorer performance in physics and chemistry may not have counted. I got through, though my rank was mediocre (1142, I remember, and for all your years in IIT that number would be stuck to you), but I got into a five-year integrated MS maths course, and very honestly I had never wanted anything else.

What was the IIT experience like, the maths and the rest? There were very few women there, weren't they, in the early eighties?

IIT Kanpur had a sprawling campus neatly laid out in a very American fashion – the roads and lanes and even hostels had numbers, not names. We were repeatedly told how we were the 'cream of the nation'– the toppers from all over the country thrown together. The atmosphere was intensely competitive and the schedule harrowing – quizzes, 'mid-sems', 'end-sems', projects, practicals . . . But for those of us who cared less about grades and wanted only to learn, there was a huge, well-stocked library, some excellent professors who were a delight to listen to, and some good friends to 'mug' (study) with. IITK was cruel to those who didn't 'fit in'. Like those who came from non-English-speaking backgrounds and had to do 'slow pace' classes; or the PhD students, derisively called

Phuds, who were generally from smaller cities and towns. The semester we joined, I remember being part of a silent angry procession of students mourning the suicide of a Dalit student who had not been able to complete his final semester.

And of course, among the minorities were the girls! In 1979 we were considered a 'big batch' of girls – we were 8 among a class of 250 boys. In some batches there were just two or three. I remember all of us as 'freshers' going to a Friday evening film show in the auditorium, ignoring the words of caution from our seniors. The moment there was a hint of sex in the film, the entire crowd went berserk – hooting, cat-calling, forcing the projection assistant to rewind. We walked out of that concentrated mix of lust and misogyny in twenty minutes flat . . . We girls were often subjected to pranks – someone taking the air out of our bicycle tyres, an anonymous note or some graffiti. But within a couple of semesters, most of the women would pair up with someone, and then after that there would be this quite liberal acceptance of the couple, with the women even staying over in the men's hostels. The girls' hostel was a really friendly zone. Unlike the competitive atmosphere of the men's hostels, which were structured by year, at the GH we had seniors and juniors and PhD students all mixed together. There was always a mature shoulder to cry on or someone to help with tough assignments.

When did you realize you would not be going the way of other IIT graduates?

I learnt a lot at IITK – and not all of it was academic. Though, of course, thanks to Professors U.B. Tewari, Kalyan Bannerji,

A.P. Shukla and V.K. Deshpande, my foundation in science and mathematics was well laid. We also had excellent teachers in the humanities, and fortunately it was compulsory for all IITK students to take a humanities course each semester – hopefully it made them less technocratic. So there were Professors Vinod Jairath, Mohini Mallick and Leelavati Krishnan teaching us sociology, philosophy and psychology. But I learnt the most from a little Marxist study group of students and teachers with whom we visited flood-devastated villages in nearby Unnao, participated in cultural programmes of the mess workers of IITK and learnt about the hardships of textile workers of the closed mills of Kanpur city. We studied about the freedom movement and the trade union movement; about how science and technology was impacting society; about the public sector and implications of the impending privatization. I began to understand that the substance of development was to be sought not in the balance sheets of companies but in the living standard of the working people. That was when I realized that I was not cut out to be an academic. I needed to be with the people and be a part of their everyday struggles.

It was this conviction that led to my surrendering my American nationality after I finished my studies at IIT Kanpur, and I can proudly say I have a certificate of Indianness issued by the home ministry itself! I did not bother afterwards to apply for a passport. I still don't have one. I shall never forget the look of disbelief on the face of the consul of the American Embassy when I told him I was quite certain I wished to renounce my American citizenship. It took his staff a week to find the form I needed to fill.

What were the other things that put you on the path to Dalli Rajhara (in present-day Chhattisgarh) to work with Niyogi?

The Asian Games were held in Delhi in 1982 and the entire city was being dug up and constructed – flyovers, stadia, five-star hotels ... Migrant workers were being brought from the poorer areas in the countryside and housed in huge camps. There was one enclosed in barbed wire close to the gate of JNU, where the Sidharth Hotel stands today. A group of students – some from JNU, some medical students from the All India Institute of Medical Sciences – wanted to support the struggles of workers. We reached out to the university staff, to the textile workers in the Delhi Cloth Mills and Birla Mill, to workers in the neighbouring Ballabgarh industrial belt and to the mostly Odiya migrant workers in the construction camp. The medical students ran medical camps and we tried to teach the children. We used to bring out a hand-printed wall newspaper, *Meri Teri Uski Baat*, named after a novel by the progressive Hindi writer Yashpal. One day, an Odiya worker we were interacting with at the camp, who had told us about the terrible conditions of bondage he, his sick wife and children were being subjected to, disappeared suddenly without a trace. This is when we began to understand the cruel power structure that underlies this misery. For me it was a revelation: no part-time charity would work. As the playwright and poet Bertolt Brecht famously said, one could not have 'a pass in his pocket' to leave these workers whenever one wished after exposing them to risk. Trade unionism demanded a life of commitment.

It was the workers of the textile mills who introduced us to Comrade Niyogi, around 1983–84. He had just then been arrested under the National Security Act and the workers were holding demonstrations for his release. We students joined the campaign. I remember going to JNU and to Delhi University professors and other prominent citizens to collect signatures on a petition for his release. When Niyogiji was finally released and he came to Delhi for a discussion with the Textiles Minister, he was curious to meet this young group of students and invited us to Dalli Rajhara, a mining township that supplied the Bhilai Steel Plant with iron ore. It was the headquarters of the Chhattisgarh Mines Shramik Sangh (CMSS), the union Niyogiji founded to fight for the rights of exploited iron ore miners.

And you went?

Yes. I shall never forget the first impact Dalli Rajhara had on me. It was 19 December 1983 – Shaheed Veer Narayan Divas, commemorating the Adivasi chieftain who had led a guerrilla struggle against the British in 1857 on the day he was supposed to have been publicly executed in Raipur town. By the time we reached Dalli Rajhara, a procession had started from the union office to encircle the town and return. It was so huge that people were still setting out when others had gone the whole way round. The impact of seeing so many barefoot peasants from the nearby villages, the miners smartly marching in their red-and-green uniform, helmets and boots, the baskets of steaming rice that were being dunked in and taken out from the iron tubs filled with boiling water, lines of people sitting down to eat the simple rice and vegetable meal on leaves woven with twigs, was like being enveloped in a warm embrace of the working people.

The CMSS was a different kind of union, one that ran schools and a hospital, had got thousands of miners to quit alcohol, and which now, after many tough struggles, had made the iron ore miners of Dalli Rajhara the highest-paid contract miners in the country. Its red–green flag spelt out a worker–peasant solidarity, and indeed the organization was active in hundreds of forest villages around the mining town, where it was known as the Chhattisgarh Mukti Morcha (CMM). It fought corrupt forest officials and moneylenders and built ponds. My mind had been made up. I had come home.

And you jumped in?

My association with the CMM began in 1984 with comings and goings from Delhi, as I tried to convince my mother about this plunge that I was planning to take. I began with teaching children in Dalli Rajhara, but Niyogiji soon asked me to work in Bhilai, where a movement of contract workers was beginning to swell in the industrial area around the Bhilai Steel Plant, consisting mostly of its private ancillaries and auxiliaries. There were no labour laws to speak of there, nor any unions; wages were a pittance; work was long and hard and unsafe. The workers wanted working conditions comparable to those of the permanent workers of the Bhilai Steel Plant. This struggle for permanency and a 'living wage' in 1991 was in fact swimming against the tide of liberalization, privatization and globalization. The movement of thousands of contract workers from scores of medium and small industrial units broke out like a river in high spate, and we became immersed to our necks in it.

What work did you do?

For nearly fourteen years or more in the CMM, I was a jack of all trades sort of karyakarta (activist), doing whatever was needed – a follower, someone in the background. During the peak of the Bhilai movement, each day would bring a new crisis. So, typing a press release, sweeping the office, maintaining a file of newspaper cuttings, translating documents, cooking food, liaising with lawyers, having meetings with women workers – there was always so much to be done, and always urgently. Sometimes there were periods of lull, as there always are in movements, and like any middle-class person one would then feel a little insecure – what am I doing? Are we achieving anything? But there was one lesson that I learnt over time. For the workers, there is little concept of individual identity. It is the union that gives them everything – their identity, their pride, their courage, their hope of a future. Yes, there are revolutionary times when civilizational changes happen in a matter of years, but generally, historical change is a very slow process. As intellectuals, our minds can leap centuries and continents in a moment, but that's not how real change works, and as Karl Marx famously said, 'The point, however, is to change it.' Slow or fast, for the workers there is no choice but to fight. They taught me patience and perseverance and a lot about not thinking that one was the centre of the world.

How did your work in Bhilai turn out?

The Bhilai movement was crushed brutally. Four thousand two hundred workers were thrown out of the companies where they had dared to form unions and demand the barest minimum – an eight-hour workday, a living wage, payment slips and gate passes, Employees' State Insurance and Provident Fund coverage. There were attacks on leaders, and subsequently the assassination of Comrade Niyogi on 28 September 1991 within two weeks of his having petitioned the President and Prime Minister. Then the brutal police firing of 1 July 1992 on a Rail Roko Satyagraha that left seventeen workers dead. Hundreds of workers were in jail, dozens in hospital. Our offices were sealed and we finally 'broke' the curfew in the bastis by coming out on 15 August to unfurl the national flag. This period exists in my memory as a blur of rushing around courts and hospitals and jails. I was so easily recognizable in my salwar-kurta that I shifted to wearing a sari, which I continued to do till I was arrested and taken to Yerawada in 2018.

How did things change after Niyogi's death?

After his death there were internal splits and divisions in the organization in 1993 and 1995 – personally, they were even more painful than the attacks by the capitalists and their police. I was now in a relationship, and my partner and I had shifted back to Dalli Rajhara. By this time I had rooted myself well among my working-class friends and their families, and it seemed only natural to start a family of one's own. However, in 1993 I suffered a terrible miscarriage during the eighth month of my pregnancy, and as Dr Saibal Jana of the Shaheed Hospital run by the CMM says, I would have gone 'the Smita Patil way' (referring to the actress who died in Mumbai from complications following childbirth) in any big city. I owe my second chance at life to the miners of Dalli Rajhara. Dozens of workers lined up to give me the blood I was rapidly losing. And then, in 1996, we adopted Maaysha, eight months old then, and brought her home; or rather, she came and made our house a home. Till she was about four, I was mostly a mother and a housewife in our little kaccha house and back garden with guava trees and a well. When she came, the union constructed a toilet for us – it was no longer possible to leave her to go to relieve oneself in the fields, remembering to take a stick along to shoo away the scavenging pigs! Thanks to Maaysha, we always had the neighbourhood children milling around at home, and my job would be to make parathas for them and dress her and her little friends up in 'saris' made of towels.

In these years I also passed my law exams, with the aid of kunjis (popular guidebooks), I admit, and in 2000, at the ripe old age of thirty-nine, I became a lawyer.

Why did you do this?

The main reason for doing a law degree was that by then I was one of the persons consistently dealing with legal matters on behalf of the CMM – first in the Niyogi murder case, then with the Bhilai Police Firing Enquiry Commission and then the cases in industrial courts, of workers of different companies in Bhilai who had been retrenched. Many wonderful lawyers appeared pro bono for us in the criminal and writ matters – Indira Jaising, Nandita Haksar, Vrinda Grover – and it's no accident that they were all women. In a historic sessions court judgment, two industrialists and their five henchmen were convicted for Niyogiji's murder. (Sadly, this was overturned in the higher courts, and eventually only one hired killer was convicted.)

When it came to labour matters, we had a tough job coping with the fees and tantrums of labour lawyers (with the honourable exception of Shri Sujoy Paul, who was an exemplary labour lawyer and is now a sitting judge of the Madhya Pradesh High Court), and looking at the battery of well-heeled corporate lawyers on the other side, what was the choice? As my comrades would say, 'Didi, anyway you do so much of the work of the lawyers yourself, why don't you just become one and save us some money?' In the year 2000, armed with my law degree and our four-year-old daughter, we moved back into Labour Camp, Jamul, in the Bhilai Industrial Estate, to a new phase of trade union life.

What has been the most satisfying part of your work as a lawyer?

The year 2007 was a watershed in many ways. The cases of the workers in the Bhilai movement had by now travelled to the high court at Bilaspur, so I began assisting a very experienced constitutional lawyer, Senior Advocate Kanak Tiwari, in representing those matters. That was when I realized that it was not only the workers who needed an empathetic lawyer; all people's movements had the same dire need. Those who needed legal help the most could afford it the least. The formal legal aid services were not only most inadequate, but they were also designed to help individuals, not groups. The laws that gave people rights – the Forest Rights Act, the labour laws, the laws protecting Dalits, Adivasis or women – were as a rule poorly implemented. On the other hand, the moment people would protest or agitate about this, the 'law and order' regime would kick in, and leaders and karyakartas would face exaggerated and fabricated criminal charges.

It was to provide legal support, both in 'offence' and 'defence' to groups – trade unions, village communities, NGOs – that I started the Janhit People's Legal Resource Centre. For the next decade, Janhit did maybe a hundred-odd cases: for villagers opposing acquisition of their lands for coal mining or power plants; for gram sabhas demanding implementation of forest rights; for communities facing environmental devastation; and for workers fighting for decent wages, safety and the right to form unions.

We met some remarkably brave clients. There was Janki Sidar, who fought Monnet Ispat Ltd against all odds for a decade to get back the land she had been fraudulently dispossessed of; Kanhai Patel and Karam Singh of Kosampali village, who battled a third round of land acquisition of their lands for the Jindal power plant and saved their village from being mined on all four sides, not to mention underground; Jangsay Poya, who faced a civil suit for lakhs of rupees foisted on him by South Eastern Coalfields Ltd for disrupting mining one day by taking a procession of villagers demanding to see the mandatory Gram Sabha Resolution granting permission for the mine; sixty-year-old Kashiram Yadav, who challenged the mighty Prakash Industries to pay up a decade of Provident Fund dues to hundreds of railway-siding loaders and almost succeeded; Bhagwati Sahu and Lakhan Sahu, who went to jail on false charges framed by a security officer of Ambuja Cement only because they organized the contract workers there to demand minimum wages . . .

In a decade we had filed cases not only against these companies but also against Balco (Vedanta), Bhilai Steel Plant, ACC, Tata, Essar, Vandana Power, Adani, National Mineral Development Corporation . . . I and our tiny team of lawyers had begun to make powerful enemies.

But 2007 was also the year the CMM faced its biggest split. Our faction was expelled and renamed itself 'CMM (Mazdoor Karyakarta Samiti)'. In dealing with this organizational turmoil, personal differences with my partner also came to a head and we decided to go our separate ways. On 14 May 2007, Dr Binayak Sen was arrested. He was a medical doctor and a human rights activist, serving as general secretary of the Chhattisgarh unit of the People's Union for Civil Liberties (PUCL). He was punished for having organized a team of human rights organizations from all over the country to investigate allegations of the emptying out of 644 villages and hundreds of killings in Bastar by a State-sponsored counter-insurgency campaign called Salwa Judum. The team had brought out a report called 'When the State Makes War on Its People'. (Much later, on 5 July 2011, the Supreme Court was to pass a landmark judgment in *Nandini Sundar & Ors vs State of Chhattisgarh & Ors*, outlawing and disbanding the Salwa Judum and vindicating the report.) When Dr Sen was arrested, I had been in the PUCL for some time but had not been at the forefront of its activities. As the chilling effect of Dr Sen's arrest hit civil society in Chhattisgarh, a handful of PUCL activists, including Dr Lakhan Singh, Shri Rajendra Sail, Ms Zulaikha Jabeen and I struggled to keep the human rights discourse alive. Gradually, PUCL not only revived but grew in strength and diversity, taking up issues of human trafficking, attacks on minorities, suppression of journalists, and fake encounters and sexual violence in counter-insurgency operations. As the general secretary of the Chhattisgarh PUCL for two terms after Dr Sen, I was bound to have earned the State's wrath.

You've said you never missed the English-speaking metropolitan world while living for decades in Chhattisgarh – apart from the urge to read the odd P.G. Wodehouse? Is

giving up the old life something you felt you had to do to be a genuine activist?

Once again, Brecht's lovely poem comes to mind. It goes something like,

> *Fighters are poor people. They cannot leave . . .*
> *Before we go into battle I must know: have you a pass*
> *In your coat pocket?*

It is not so much about giving up the old life. I have found the working class quite accepting, even of activists who are culturally quite alien, if they trust their sincerity. It is about not leaving. It is about staying on even when the situation is grim. And you can stay only when you take root, when you feel comfortable, when you make friends. Coming from a middle-class, intellectual background, from a nuclear family with a single atheist feminist mother and a British childhood to boot, it was initially a big chasm to bridge, socially and culturally. But the time came when I really began to feel at home sitting in my doorway in the labour camp, chatting with my neighbours as we cleaned some bhaaji and our children dozed in our laps. I always enjoyed the night-long Chhattisgarhi naacha (folk theatre) programmes in the villages, where everyone sat on gunnysacks wrapped up in shawls and laughed at the sly political banter of the jester and waited for the sun to rise. And I began to confide my most personal troubles to my working-class comrades. Yes, of course, I would still miss playing Scrabble with my mother or reading a P.G. Wodehouse, and there's nothing wrong with that – it just meant one learnt to straddle both worlds.

You've said you consider yourself a leftist and a Marxist, and that you are very sceptical about capitalism. Why?

The first reason is that I have seen the underbelly of that capitalism from very close quarters – the condition of the migrant construction workers who toiled to make the stadia for the Asian Games; the contract workers who died in accidents in the Bhilai Steel Plant or Ambuja Cement for completely avoidable reasons; the houses and fields of Chhurikala village in Korba caked in the fly ash of surrounding thermal power plants; or the poverty of the Adivasis displaced by the Bailadila mines where the rivers run red with iron ore; and the callousness the companies and the State displayed when it came to legitimate demands for better wages, safe working conditions, mitigation of environmental degradation or adequate compensation and rehabilitation for land acquisition. Second, the obscenely growing gap between the rich and the poor. We are told that growth is going to 'trickle down' one day, but I see it 'gushing up' into Mauritian tax havens. The 2023 Oxfam Report, aptly titled 'Survival of the Richest', has found that just 5 per cent of Indians own more than 60 per cent of the country's wealth, while the bottom 50 per cent of the population has only 3 per cent of it.

A system that uses the labour of multitudes and generates enormous wealth but does not distribute it. A system that possesses cutting-edge medical knowledge and still allows people to die from malnutrition, TB, gastroenteritis and malaria. A system that is scientifically and technologically highly advanced and yet insists on degrading the environment of this planet so much as to make it unlivable. A system that breeds war, colonial occupation and fascism. That is what modern-day capitalism is.

No doubt the socialist experiments of the Soviet Union and China, after the initial spectacular leaps ahead in living conditions, ended in the stranglehold of single-party-led State capitalism too. But surely that is no reason not to keep trying to achieve socialism, because the world in its present condition is not one human beings deserve.

Can you be called a dissident?

If that means do I dare speak against corporates, against governments, against powerful people when they are tyrannical? . . . Yes. But I also believe that I am a deeply Constitution-abiding person. I have striven for and will continue to strive for justice, liberty, equality and fraternity for every citizen around me. Is that dissidence?

After three decades in Chhattisgarh, you moved to Delhi, became a visiting professor at the National Law University (NLU). This was a big move. Why did you do it?

Around June 2017, I began to feel strongly that Maaysha had entered a critical phase in her life and education. She needed my time and attention. I also needed to be able to provide for her to go to a good college. Till then I had devoted myself entirely to my work in Chhattisgarh – to CMM, to Janhit and to PUCL, without a thought of earning, let alone saving anything. So I gratefully accepted the offer of a visiting professorship at NLU, Delhi – my first formal 'job', at the age of fifty-six.

Did you like the work? What was it, what part of it did you enjoy? What sort of students did you have?

I loved teaching at NLU, Delhi. I taught part of a course on law and poverty, gave a few lectures on labour law, and designed and taught a course called 'Evolution of Laws in Interface with People's Movements' for final-year students. The course was about how and why the Forest Rights Act of 2006 and the new Land Acquisition Act of 2013 came into existence, and the role that people's movements played in shaping them. I really enjoyed interacting with my students (who included at one point a group of trainee officers from the Central Reserve Police Force) – answering their queries, discussing with them how to research topics of their interest, and listening to them present their papers in groups. There might have been a few who were bored or non-serious or who attended only for the sake of grades, but by and large I found them an enthusiastic lot, keen to delve deep and to argue, and eager to really help people in some way. It makes me sad to think that many of these promising young people will finally end up in corporate firms, only because they need to repay loans or to get better salaries, and that they will probably abandon litigation altogether. Legal aid is, of course, out of the question as a career choice, and yet they were so interested in the Janhit sort of experiment.

What was yours and Maaysha's life like in Faridabad? More broadly, what have you learnt from being Maaysha's mother?

Any person in public life pays for it in the most painful way by not having enough time and mental space for their family. Maaysha's desire to have a normal home and a normal family was a deep ache inside her being. The love and care with which she decorated and managed our home in Faridabad spoke eloquently of that. Though I had a long commute by metro, nearly two hours point to point, to reach NLU, it was lovely to come home to a cup of tea, watch some serial together in the evening – my favourite was *Sa Re Ga Ma Pa*, the children's music contest – and just be with her. It was she who taught me that I needed this, to step back a little, for myself as much as for her. While she successfully completed her tenth and twelfth courses from the National Institute of Open Schooling, it was in Delhi that the diabetes that I had already probably been living with for years was diagnosed. I started listening to music again and reading widely and watching films – things I hadn't done in a while. Unfortunately, that normality was to be short-lived.

When did you first hear of the criminal case in which you have been implicated? What was your reaction?

My bail conditions specify that I cannot speak publicly about the proceedings in my case, so I will answer this question in general terms. The first I heard about the case was when someone called me in early July and told me to watch Republic TV as I was being ranted about there . . . I was shocked and served a defamation notice on the channel and its editor and anchor, Arnab Goswami. I made a public statement in my defence, and I was fortunate in that both the students and a good number of faculty members of NLU supported me. I was anxious, but actually it seemed more Kafkaesque than anything else – sort of unreal and illogical.

There was a knock on the door, and shortly afterwards you were put under house arrest. Policewomen lived with you for weeks. When you look back at that time, what do you remember?

The date is etched in my memory – 28 August 2018. It must have been around 7 a.m. when I answered the door in a nightie. It was a posse of policemen and policewomen from Pune, mostly in civil dress, except the awkward-looking woman constable from the Suraj Kund police station they had brought along. I changed into a sari and went to wake Maaysha up and tell her the cops were here. I sat on the sofa hugging a rather subdued and scared Maaysha while the cops went through the cupboards, books and stuff in the bedrooms.

Just then Rosie, my young domestic help, came to the door. She scolded the policeman who was telling her to go away, 'Arre, how can Didi manage without me? Let me in!' Viva la working class! And in she came, and we offered everybody tea. After a long time, after formalities had been completed, the officer in charge told my daughter: 'Don't worry, we are just taking her to the nearby police station. Our Sahab is sitting there and he will ask her a few questions, that's all.'

At the Suraj Kund police station I was told that I was being arrested. I informed Maaysha over the telephone and she began to cry. The news had spread. My friends Professor Jayati Ghosh and Smita Gupta had come to the police station, and a much-loved activist of the National Alliance for People's Movements (NAPM), Vimal bhai, had come too. I did not know Vimal bhai well at that time though he lived fairly close to my house, but he was to prove a pillar of support to Maaysha later.

Now, transit remand had to be obtained to take me to Pune. I was brought to the Faridabad court, and we found the Chief Judicial Magistrate (CJM) gone off to a condolence meeting. The President of the District Bar Association came to represent me. Other advocate friends – Shalini Gera, Monu Kuhar and Madhur Bharatiya – arrived as well. When I was produced before a very competent and stern young woman judicial magistrate first class, I was impressed. It took them the whole day to try and satisfy her pertinent queries.

Meanwhile, our lawyers in the Punjab and Haryana High Court (Faridabad, though on the outskirts of Delhi, is in Haryana state), secured a stay on transit remand until a petition filed in the Supreme Court by five prominent intellectuals, led by Romila Thapar and Prabhat Patnaik, pertaining to the arrests of five people, including myself, was heard two days later. I had learned by then that besides me, poet Varavara Rao, lawyer Arun Fereira, human rights activist Gautam Navlakha and columnist Vernon Gonsalves had all been arrested the same day in Hyderabad, Delhi and Mumbai.

I shall never forget the high drama of that night. In filmi style, the Pune police had whisked me into a car and we were hurtling towards the airport. I could hear the flurry of excited phone calls the officer in my car was receiving. Finally, it was a call from the SHO of Suraj Kund police station, quoting the Registrar of the Punjab and Haryana High Court, which made him turn around and bring me back to the CJM's house. It was past 1 a.m. when my house arrest order was signed and 2 a.m. when I was brought home to a tearful Maaysha.

The house arrest lasted two months as the Supreme Court case was being heard. Women of Haryana Police were deputed to guard me. Having them outside our flat on the third floor would mean the entire building would be under surveillance and its residents harassed. Besides, they were women and the nights were cold. So finally, I suggested that four of them could 'guard' me by occupying my sitting room and sleeping in turns in one of our two bedrooms. No one except my advocates and the belligerent Rosie were permitted to enter, and their names were meticulously recorded in a register. I was not allowed to use a phone, and the door to Maaysha's bedroom, where the two of us slept, had to be kept open and the balcony door locked. It was so claustrophobic an arrangement that Maaysha preferred to be away at friends' houses. But I eventually made friends with the police ladies, who would pass the time watching TV, finishing their duty notes or even babysitting their children telephonically. Some curious one in almost every batch would unfailingly ask me, 'So Madam, what exactly is your case?' – a question to which truthfully I really had no answer.

You smile in some photographs taken around that time. Is that your reflexive way of responding to stress, to not let it show? Or your strong belief that tomorrow will be better?

Oh yes, the famous photo in front of the Suraj Kund police station with Vimal bhai. In a Kafkaesque situation what else can one do but laugh? One is powerless to resist, but one can still have dignity and courage if one believes truth is on one's side.

Describe your last day at home, with Maaysha, before you were arrested and flown to Pune and placed in the Faraskhana lock-up where your diary begins. What were your feelings as you left? What did you think of on the journey?

We would watch the ticker on NDTV with bated breath on the days when my case was being heard in the Supreme Court. And Advocate Vrinda Grover, my lawyer and old friend, or one of her colleagues, would come by in the evening to give us a blow-by-blow account of what had transpired. Eventually, on 28 September 2018 (did it have to be the day of Comrade Niyogi's martyrdom?), the Supreme Court decided against us – in a two-to-one verdict. The dissenting judgment was written by the present Chief Justice of India D.Y. Chandrachud. I was given four weeks to approach the Pune Sessions Court for bail. Advocate Yug Chaudhary, who represented me later in the high court, argued the bail on my behalf. Predictably, it was rejected, and my four weeks were up on 26 October 2018.

Maaysha would hate to see me pack my little bag with two sets of clothes, my medicines and a book before every court hearing. 'You seem to want to go,' she blurted out angrily one day. Being prepared was my way of accepting the inevitable without drama. But within me I felt terrible about leaving her to experience the pain of abandonment yet another time in her young life. The night before 27 October, I hardly slept. I had asked Maaysha to get me salwar-kurtas for my future life of confinement, and I donned the new khadi kurta she had got me. Early in the morning, the Haryana policewomen told me the cops from Pune had arrived the night before and would be coming soon. Mother and daughter spent a silent half-hour just hugging one another – what was one to say? The ever-dependable Rosie was there, crying and promising me she would look after Maaysha Didi. A crowd of my friends had gathered downstairs with placards, but I could only wave as I was hurriedly pushed into the waiting police vehicle. There were OB vans at the gate of the colony and people looked curiously on – what sort of celebrity is this? The airport and the flight are a blur in my mind. I only recall thinking – what a waste of public money! But I remember distinctly the smart and confident young lawyer who came up to me in the Pune Sessions Court and introduced himself as Rahul Deshmukh. It was reassuring to shake hands with him – a friend in a strange city that was going to be my address for the year to come. He informed me that ten days' police custody had been granted by the court. The ordeal had begun in earnest.

How This Book Came to Be Written

The jottings which make up this book were my way of coping with incarceration. Some prisoners pray, some weep, some just put their heads down and work themselves weary. Some fight defiantly every inch of the way, some are inveterate grumblers, some spew gossip. Some read the newspaper from cover to cover, some shower love on children, some laugh at themselves and at others.

I watched through the bars, and I wrote.

These notes were written during the first half of my incarceration; that is, during my time in the Yerawada Women's Jail, Pune, between early November 2018 and late February 2020. I wrote them in my cell at night, in notebooks that I bought from the jail Canteen. And when I was shifted to Byculla Jail, Mumbai, I took them with me. I typed them out after my release on bail in December 2021.

Except for the first week, I spent my entire time at Yerawada in the Phansi Yard (death row) of the Women's Jail, where my co-accused in the Bhima Koregaon case, Professor Shoma Sen, and I were lodged in neighbouring single cells. We were never told why we were in this high-security unit for death-row prisoners, but it probably had something to do with our being arrested under the draconian Unlawful Activities (Prevention) Act (UAPA). I could take ten paces down the length of my cell and six paces across its width, and indeed I did a lot of pacing about. Our neighbours in the Yard were two highly strung sisters, lodged in similar separate cells, who had by then entered their twenty-fourth year in jail, of which nearly two decades had been spent on death row. These four cells and a fifth vacant cell (used as a storeroom and bathroom by the Constables guarding us 24x7), and the narrow corridor into which they opened, were all enclosed in a cage-like structure, with bars all along the front. The cage lay along half the longer side of a rectangular grassy ground, overlooking it. The other half of that side, to our left, was taken up by the Hospital Barrack. Barracks 1 and 2, housing mostly convicts, stood on the adjacent (shorter) side of the rectangle, to our right, and their windows overlooked the ground too.

Ours was a cage with a view. Through its bars we could see the sparse, well-worn lawn where women prisoners ate their lunch and played with their children, and could hear the sermons delivered by the visiting Brahma Kumaris (preachers from a spiritual organization) on the raised cement Stage right in front of our cage. We could observe the goings-on at the far end of the ground, such as women at the prison Gate leaving for courts or for the hospital, lining up at the Dispensary or waiting to enter the Mulakat (meeting) Room to meet their visitors. We could watch the older children playing on the see-saw, swings and slide, and see women crossing over from our 'Convict Compound' to the adjoining 'Undertrial Compound'. (These were not tightly sealed categories. There were undertrials – like us – in the Convict Compound, and the other way around.) The two compounds were separated by a high wall and a massive iron-sheeted gate towards the far end of the ground on the left. We could watch women covered in plastic sheets in the monsoon, lining up at the Gate to go to work in the open fields next to the prison. Even the window at the back of our cell had a view. If you stood on the raised platform where the Indian-style toilet was fitted, you saw the Factory where women stitched blouses, wove strips of dhurries and rolled agarbattis; and also the shed of a company called Spark Minda, where the younger, more educated prisoners went, wearing smart white jackets over their prison clothes, to manufacture small auto parts.

We were not supposed to interact with other prisoners. In fact, Professor Sen and I usually spent sixteen and a half out of twenty-four hours in our adjoining individual cells. The wall separating us had a small window near the roof so one could shout to each other in an emergency. For a few hours each day, we were let out into the narrow corridor outside our cells. In the winter we were let out of our cage for half an hour between 12 noon and 12.30 to 'take the sun', and later on this practice continued. This was a time when no other prisoners were out and about since everyone was locked up in their barracks between 12 noon and 3 p.m.

So, how and when did I learn the stories of other women? When we huddled together in the police van en route to court, or spent hours cooped up in the paan-stained court lock-up waiting to be summoned to our respective courts. When we queued up outside the Mulakat Room, each anxious to meet her family and lawyers. When we lined up outside the Dispensary and commiserated over each other's aches and pains, or waited outside the Canteen to get our supplies for the fortnight. When we jostled at the common tap to fill bottles of drinking water and buckets for bathing and for washing clothes, under the eagle eye of our Constable on guard. When we heard our Constable on duty chit-chat with other passing prisoners or a colleague. Sometimes our neighbours, the two sisters, would tell us stories too, when they were in a rare, pleasant mood. And there was no way we could be deaf to the fights in Barracks 1 or 2 or in the Hospital Barrack – the loud sounds of crying or cursing inevitably spilled out into the corridors and the ground.

I like trying to put myself in someone else's shoes. Sometimes, watching through the bars, a woman would catch my eye, and then I would keep filing away in my mind the little details I would observe about her over many chance meetings. Once the pieces fell into place, like a jigsaw puzzle, I would write about her. Similarly, I would piece together my observations on jail life: the things that amused me, moved me, frustrated me, horrified me, made me mull over solutions. That is why my notes have no dates and no particular chronology. There are also no dates because jail life is like a grindstone, just turning and turning, with an unchanging routine. The passage of time is measured only by the changes of season and festivals. Besides, I had told myself that I should not expect to be released soon. I wanted to protect myself from the emotional rollercoaster of hope and despair every time a bail application was filed and rejected.

My prison notes are impressionistic snapshots, true to the moment, with no claim to being complete histories. I have omitted names to protect the privacy of these prisoners and avoid prejudice to their cases. Observing women, listening to them, writing about them, and about life in a women's jail, helped me. This became my work. It gave me a sense of purpose. It calmed me. It helped me understand where I was, and didn't leave any scope for self-pity!

As a trade unionist for more than three decades and a human rights lawyer for nearly two, it is not as if I was unaware of the injustices prisoners were subjected to, and their sufferings. I knew many laws were unreasonable, even draconian. I knew that the quality of legal aid was poor. I knew that the actions of courts were often prejudiced against the poor, the Dalits and the minorities. I knew that courts looked at crimes within the family through a patriarchal lens. But being in prison made one understand the enormity of it all, the serious implications of these things on real human lives. And above all, the urgency for reform.

This is not to say that all the women were 'innocent' or had not committed crimes. I did find, though, when I heard their stories, that a good number seemed to have been lured or forced or provoked into such crimes by their circumstances. In a more enlightened society than ours, the attitude towards crime would not be one of revenge or punishment, but of reform and rehabilitation. So I have, in my sketches of them, tried to treat these women not as criminals but as human beings. I remember once in Byculla, when I was asked to sing – and I have a very loud singing voice – I sang '*Voh subah kabhi toh aayegi*' (Some day, that morning will dawn), written by the poet Sahir Ludhianvi and sung in a Hindi film. When I came to the lines, '*Jailon ke bina is duniya ki, sarkar chalayi jayegi*' (One day the world will be governed without jails), not a single eye was dry.

In this book, I have tried to tell the stories of some of the women of Yerawada Jail as I saw them in the space of a year and a couple of months that I was there. Days, as I have said, dissolve into each other there, but the seasons you notice and experience. They worsen your discomforts, sending you scrambling for precious water, petitioning for a fan or trying to shelter yourself from the chilly air coming in through the bars. They also soothe you, rejuvenate you and make you more aware of the natural world than if you were 'outside'. I have introduced each section of the book with a few passages on my own experiences from one season to the next, after which follow my prison notes.

Among them are seventy-six portraits of women or groups of women, each of which I have numbered. They are precious to me because they encapsulate what these prisoners at Yerawada – many of them in far more difficult circumstances than I – taught me, every single day I was there. How to survive injustice, how to remain hopeful, how to help one other, and how to continue to live, love, fight and laugh . . . even behind bars.

sudha bharadwaj
Mumbai, August 2023

Winter

On 27 October 2018, my two-month-long house arrest at my home in Faridabad ends. I am flown to Pune and remanded to police custody for ten days till 6 November 2018.

The Faraskhana lock-up, attached to the Faraskhana police station in Pune city, is filthy. Cobwebs laden with black soot hang from the ceiling, the walls are smeared with paan and tobacco stains, the blankets are full of bedbugs and there is no bucket to wash away the mess in the toilets. Oh Lord, how will I survive this, I think to myself. Each day new women come and go. A kind Constable helps me get a bucket and mug. During the day I am taken to the office of the Assistant Commissioner of Police for interrogation, but there is hardly any interrogation, and somehow the ten days pass.

The evening I enter the Yerawada Women's Jail, it's dark and cold. The high walls are formidable, fortress-like. The Constables in the lobby-like space in between the outer walls and the enormous iron gate leading to the barracks, a space I later learn to call 'the Gate', roughly dump the contents of my bag on the stone floor and throw out most of my things – no T-shirts and track pants allowed, only salwar-kurta or sari, no clutchers for my hair. I am told to strip in a dingy side room – 'yes, take off everything', 'squat', 'open your hair' – under the watchful eye of an enormous tabby. I feel naked, and not just physically. Dressed again, I am handed the things that will, from now, be my basic set of worldly belongings: bedding – a patti, which is a narrow, thin dhurrie; a rough woven blanket called a ghongri; a chaddar; and my utensils – aluminium plate, bowl and mug.

My first (sleepless) night is spent in the Hospital Barrack, where I am grudgingly given a narrow place as wide as my patti near a woman nobody seems to like. With great relief, I discover that the toilet is very clean. Next morning, at 5.30 a.m., I see the rows of women sitting cross-legged on the cold stone floor for the Total, the Morning Round (yes, I am learning a whole new vocabulary), where the prisoners are counted, and join them hesitantly. 'One Maovadi,' says the yellow-sari-ed Warder, pointing me out to the morning-shift Constables who arrive, chatting and giggling. (I take her for a 'Madam', a jail official. It's only later that I realize she's a convict too.) At 7 a.m., the lock to the barrack is opened and everyone rushes out.

'Hey, you can't dry your clothes there,' a prisoner rebukes me, when I attempt to use one of the clothes lines behind the barrack. It turns out that sections of the lines have been 'booked' by various inmates. It is another taste of 'non-freedom', of the innumerable restrictions of jail life. Soon I am standing in line with all the other new admissions near the Gate, holding my Undertrial (UT) Card in front of my chest. (It's like an identity card for the jail but without a photograph and mentions the crime number and sections of the law.) The Superintendent and his retinue of subordinates move down the line, inspecting us. He lectures some in a preachy way, warning them to behave themselves. He looks closely at me, says 'Hmm', and moves on.

Things don't look so bad when the sun comes out. The one-storeyed barracks with their tiled roofs, trees and flower beds, the children playing, the women in green saris doing their morning chores . . . it could be an ashram, I tell myself. I learn later that green saris are worn by convicts or undertrials accused of murder. I try to strike up a conversation with an inmate. 'Don't ask anyone about their case. Not a done thing here,' a young woman who seems to have taken me under her wing advises me. An elderly prisoner gives me a cloth bag. 'Here, keep your clothes in it,' she says. 'Everybody has duties here – bringing the bhatta (food) on their heads and sweeping and swabbing the barrack. I will do it for you.' The unsaid part is that it's not free – one pays for someone else's labour by buying them things from the Canteen. The veterans have sized me up – middle class and naïve.

My name is being yelled from the Mulakat Room. My daughter Maaysha has arrived. She cries into the telephone as she speaks to me. We both touch the glass that separates us, trying to connect. My union colleagues accompanying her can't meet me. Prisoners jailed under the UAPA have greater restrictions on them than others. We are only allowed to meet 'blood relations' and lawyers.

I am getting used to being in the Hospital Barrack, making some friends, learning to eat the bhatta. I have even found the hiding place where the Warder keeps the Marathi paper supplied to the barrack – it gives me something to read, and I try to make sense of it. Suddenly one evening, at around 4.30 p.m., just before we are locked in, a Constable harshly orders me out with my bag. I am marched to the Phansi Yard. The Constable opens the door of a single cell. I enter, and clang – the barred gate bangs shut and is locked. For the first time since I left home, tears prick my eyes, at the unfairness of it all. I lie on the cold stone floor, not even bothering to spread my patti. Then I hear a voice asking, 'Sudha, are you okay?' from across the wall. It's Professor Shoma Sen. We know of each other but have not been intimate friends. She is sending me a bit of her dinner through the Guard on duty. I hadn't had time to collect mine. It's this friendship that is going to be our mainstay in the days to come. 'Yes I'm fine,' I shout back.

1

Young, slender, dark and doe-eyed, with thick straight hair tied in a bun. Not beautiful when examined feature by feature, but very attractive in her animated totality. Unfazed by the depressing surroundings of the Faraskhana lock-up and the harshness with which the Guards speak to us, the Maratha girl regales us with a blow-by-blow account, replete with gestures, of how she was wooed by her Tamil boyfriend, eloped with him and married him. 'People think we are boyfriend and girlfriend even now,' she says. 'I always wear jeans.' Both families are reconciled to the marriage, she tells us, adding that she is the darling of her mother-in-law. Her cheerful chatter goes on and on . . . how she loves shopping, cooking and eating out, how much her husband must be missing her . . .

Hearing her speak, I forget my own troubles and find myself completely absorbed in trying to understand the puzzle of who she is and why she is here. She sounds and behaves like a modern middle-class working girl. Could she really have been party to her married brother punishing an ex-girlfriend with rape? She says the girlfriend had cheated him of several lakhs, and so he took revenge? And she? How deep does this 'modernity' go? Still, I am relieved not to see her in jail later. Perhaps she got bail? Somehow, I can't believe that she deliberately abetted a rape ...

2

Five Nepali women enter the lock-up. Humiliating and sexually explicit abuses are hurled at them by both the female and male cops accompanying them. It turns out that they have been booked under the Prevention of Immoral Trafficking Act (PITA) for 'maintaining brothels' in a well-known lane of houses in Pune's Budhwar Peth. Initially, they stick together defiantly, these women between the ages of thirty-five and sixty and slowly, over the next seven days, they regain their dignity. One day they even clean up the dirty corridor of the lock-up with great energy. In fits and starts, these gentle, plump women tell the rest of us their stories. The oldest talks of how for decades, she went back time and again to Nepal with her earnings. First to search for her children, then to buy a little plot of land, then to build a small hut for them. Her son now works in Chennai. Another woman is distraught. 'My children, who are studying in boarding school, will read my name in the paper. They will hate me,' she says. I try to console her, 'Why should they be angry? Shouldn't they know what their mother has gone through to bring them up?'

A more aloof Nepali woman tells me, 'We are Buddhist. Here only "lower people" [she probably means Dalits] are

Buddhist . . . ' I dislike her snobbishness but only remonstrate weakly. I am in no mood to deliver lectures.

A talkative member of the group explains, 'Things were different earlier. Young girls used to be forced into the trade. But now all our girls are doing this of their own free will. Many of them are married. We just keep the house. No one stays at night. The cops take money and shoo away the customers in a raid, and we are the ones who are caught. Some twenty girls have been caught too, mostly Bengali, and sent for rehabilitation. Three of their husbands also came to court. Tell me, Ma'am, everyone knows this open secret. That so-and-so sanstha [NGO] published it in the newspaper, so the police raided us. Tell me, Ma'am, isn't this law wrong?'

Later, in Yerawada Jail, I notice that there is no end to this 'immoral' traffic. Each week, PITA 'girls', 'managers' and 'madams' arrive, leave and return. Sometimes the Nepali and Bangladeshi women find it hard to get bail, even after a bail order has been passed in their favour. They have to stay in jail for months together because no zamanatdar is available to stand surety for them.

3

She's a Dalit nurse. Her father was in the army, and after his death her mother got a cleaning job. The daughter wanted more respectable work, a nursing job in the army, but a tout asked for Rs 5 lakh and she didn't have the money. She had a bad marriage with an alcoholic and abusive husband. After his death she was molested by her jeth (husband's elder brother), but none of her in-laws believed her story. She and her two schoolgoing kids live with a man she considers her muhbola (sworn) brother and his wife, for security, since she works on night shifts. They sleep in the kitchen and tolerate the taunts of the man's wife, who doesn't like this arrangement, even though the nurse contributes her share of the living expenses.

She was working as a day nurse at a private home, but was being pressured to work nights too. So, she left that job, she tells me, and joined a hospital. Now, two months later, she has been accused by her previous employer of stealing jewellery. The police are harsh, she says, and humiliate her repeatedly.

She's a proud Ambedkarite and scoffs at the Marathas. 'They dominate us and now they are begging for reservation.' She has not told her children about her arrest and has sent them to her mother-in-law. Her daughter is very good at studies. She is strict with her but lets her son do whatever he likes – let him just pass! Her daughter wants to become a police sub-inspector. That's her own dream too, to see her daughter in a police officer's uniform. Considering how much caste discrimination there is within the police, I don't know whether to feel happy or disappointed for her.

4

On 1 November, my birthday, I stick my head out of the lock-up and request the male havildar (guard) to call a chaiwala (teaseller) so that I can treat all the staff and inmates to tea. He agrees and lets me pay the chaiwala from the money in my bag. That tea in a thimble-sized cardboard cup is the best tea of my life. And it was all her idea.

She's a Head Constable with more than twenty-five years of service, and for the last few years she has been guarding the female lock-up in the daytime. Big, dark and round, she makes the sun rise for us with her flashing smile and booming voice.

Two or three cops (mostly men) come every three hours to inspect us. Unlike the other Guards, who treat us scornfully, rudely shouting 'Uthha' (get up) and 'Zhopa' (go to sleep) several times a night when these 'Rounds' are made, she is humane.

'After all, even the accused are human beings. It's all a matter of stomach (livelihood) and fate,' she says. She gets us drinking water in bottles and hands us soaps and medicines from our bags that are hung outside the lock-up.

Why is she different? Someone could say she gets bribes for being nice, which may well be the case. But that's not explanation enough. She is an elderly Muslim woman. Maybe she has seen too much of life not to be compassionate.

5

I manage to start a few conversations in the Hospital Barrack. So many here seem to be girlfriends, wives and sisters who say they didn't know what crimes the men in their lives were committing. And those who did treated 'going along' as part of either their 'love' or their 'duty'.

A young, plump, pretty and vivacious woman is the life and soul of the barrack. Bold and coquettish, she shares sly jokes with the prisoners and jail staff, loving to cross the line. She is the favourite of the tight-lipped Warder (they are called Tai here), and also her trusted lieutenant, which earns her both privileges and resentment. The barrack has a 'Marathi group' and a 'Bengali group' that are constantly bickering with each other. She heads the former while the latter are mostly young Muslims – many of them Bangladeshi – booked under PITA.

With great frankness, she tells the story of how a gangster first stalked her relentlessly and then how she fell in love with him. And managed to keep it a secret from her husband and two sons. She dotes on her sons. 'My elder one plays football,' she says, showing me his photograph. They are with their grandmother now: 'After all, one can't trust a husband!' She has been arrested under the stringent MCOCA (Maharashtra Control of Organised Crime) Act. The gangster boyfriend murdered someone who had squealed on him. She had gone to his 'den' that day. She describes how the police tried to coerce her to name all those who were present that day, including the rickshaw-wala who ferried her to the den. She refused. 'I wouldn't get anyone stuck in a case.' How brave she is, I think, but to what end?

6

She is a big, dark woman with close-cropped hair. They say she was in a mental asylum for two years. She doesn't remember or know why she is here. 'What's your case?' '302,' she replies. This is the section under the Indian Penal Code (IPC) for murder. 'Hush,' everyone admonishes her, 'don't be silly, that's murder. If you were booked for that, you would be wearing a green sari, like the other murder undertrials.'

Is she a beggar? A thief? She can't remember. But she sometimes breaks into old Hindi film songs in a strong, tuneful voice. One arm and one leg of hers tremble like a Parkinson patient's. She eats a lot at odd times – including leftovers discarded by others. She lies down to sleep anywhere, even on the cold stone floor. Occasionally she weeps silently to go home. I hear she is on psychiatric medicines.

In their own strange way, everyone cares for her. They humour her, crack jokes, give her extra food. 'Have you eaten?' someone on the Night Round invariably asks her, while handing over her nightly psychiatric dose and checking that the prisoners are firmly locked in the barrack.

On Diwali, her barrack-mates take off the grimy sari she usually wears and dress her in a bright and shiny one.

Sometimes she says, 'I will kill the old man who got me here!' In that moment, the ferocity in her eyes is frightening, and one remembers with a start that she is a criminal. Of late she has begun telling the Constables that she hears a man abusing her from behind her barrack.

When she has to go for a check-up to the mental asylum, they fool her and tell her she is going home, and she gets ready with great enthusiasm. It's a cruel thing because it makes her even more angry and sad. I wonder, will she ever go home?

7

She's the picture of poise and dignity. Fair, slim, tall, with a long braid, dressed in a T-shirt and trackpants. She comes from her barrack in the Undertrial Compound every morning to take yoga classes in the covered Hall in one corner of our Convict Compound. In her rhythmic voice she counts from one to ten and from ten to one in Marathi as she leads exercises effortlessly from the raised platform. Encouraging an overweight person to bend further, correcting the posture of another, she walks among the rows of women, looking them over with a professional eye. I hear she was a 'bitcoin agent', a small cog in an enormous speculative machine, which the law has still not made up its mind about. Is bitcoin legal or illegal? It's six months now and no bail. She looks resigned.

8

She is an elderly Kannadiga woman suffering from psoriasis. She keeps her hands and feet – dotted with burn-like scars, covered under her green sari, the uniform, as I know well now, for the undertrials charged with murder. She is easily given to tears over the squabbles in the barrack or a scolding from the Warder, and cries each time she speaks to her younger sister in another barrack. She is in jail because her sister's daughter-in-law died in mysterious circumstances. The dead woman's father has not accused her husband of the crime, only her mother-in-law, sister-in-law and aunt-in-law. Only women have been arrested in the case.

She says she used to visit her sister's place in Pune every two months to pick up her medicine for psoriasis. This time she was persuaded to stay back and celebrate Diwali, and thus ended up being arrested. 'And this is the Diwali I got,' she says bitterly, full of self-pity.

So many unhappy women: a young one who took her own life or was forced by circumstances to do so; this older one, pining away for her family living far away – somewhere near Bengaluru – who don't visit her. Strange are the ways of the law in dealing with their sorrows . . .

9

I'm beginning to realize that many women are in jail for the alleged murders of their husbands. One of them catches my eye – a dignified upper-caste woman in her early sixties. Later I learn that she has very few visitors or money orders, and manages to buy a few biscuit packets from the Canteen by 'doing the duties' of other prisoners – that is, sweeping, swabbing the floor or bringing the bhatta to the Hospital Barrack, earning Rs 5 per duty. Each day, in each barrack, two persons are allocated these duties, and generally one's turn comes once or twice a month.

She is never idle, always busy with her crochet work, poring over it through her spectacles, clicking away at a remarkable pace, making a full-length gown in three or four days. She has got special permission for this, because needles, pins and scissors are not allowed – they may be used as weapons, after all. She earns only Rs 250 for each such crochet garment, which will fetch Rs 1,000 in the jail's Showroom after being fitted with an inner lining.

She has copied some shlokas (couplets in Sanskrit) in her notebook in a not very practised hand and sits reading them with her head covered in the cold mornings when we sit cross-legged in a line awaiting the Total. Rarely speaking to others, she pads barefoot to the BC (that's what the jail kitchen is called, but I have no idea why) to bring the bhatta in the large aluminium vessels carried on one's head.

Only sometimes, when she sits with all the others watching TV, always crocheting, does she hum a film song under her breath. It's so easy to transpose this figure to a middle-class drawing room among children and grandchildren that to see her here feels surreal.

She has a literary bent of mind, helps people select books in the library, and is an avid reader herself. After my transfer to the Phansi Yard, when I bump into her as we collect hot water from the solar heater, she says she won a chess competition.

In a rare talkative mood while lending me a bag to keep my stuff in, she tells me how she sat on a hunger strike in another, smaller jail along with a few male prisoners because the jail staff would siphon off whatever eatables relatives brought for them. (There was no Canteen in that jail.) Of course, that's why she was transferred here, and she says many prisoners cried when she left. So she is quite the satyagrahi.

The woman also has a sister who is the co-accused in her case, and she – the sister – has been arrested for the murder of her own husband as well. I try to imagine what cruel criminal mind might lie behind that cultured and disciplined exterior but fail.

10

She's the one who gives me a place to sleep next to her when I first enter the Hospital Barrack. Perhaps no one else wants to sleep next to her, but I for one am grateful for her acceptance. I get to know her better in the next few days. She is dark with large eyes, has dark patches on her cheeks, which I recognize as a sign of malnutrition. She ties her rough, uncombed, brownish hair in a ponytail. She wears a gaudy sari that someone has given her and walks with a pronounced limp. One leg seems to be impaired, by polio perhaps? She is a great cribber and weeper, forever complaining of all sorts of aches and pains, which are no doubt real enough for her but which nobody has the patience to deal with any more. She is also a 'borrower-and-never-returner'.

She ran away from her husband with a lover whom she claims has got her 'stuck here' in a case of kidnapping of children. 'Tell me,' she asks, '*he* took the child and gave him to me, shouldn't *he* be punished?' He is in the Main Jail, apparently ill, and writes her plaintive postcards asking her to meet him in the monthly jail mulakats that are permitted between the women and their male co-accused family members. The letters, which she makes me read out, end with many 'I love yous', to my great embarrassment. But at the end of each letter she is unmoved and says, 'I don't care about him, I want to get out.'

She sometimes weeps, though, when a particularly soppy Bollywood movie like *Hum Dil De Chuke Sanam* is playing. Sometimes she will look at the ads of models in the barrack newspaper and say, to my great surprise, 'Don't you think I look as beautiful as her?' It's difficult to say whether she is really so mentally out of touch with reality that she believes this, or is simply joking. She limps to the agarbatti factory to earn something occasionally, but is erratic in her attendance. Lately she has acquired a Bible, which she can't read but she prays before it.

She has great pride in her eight-year-old daughter, who she says is 'very pretty and fair'. The jail grapevine claims that the child is not hers. The child is in a sanstha and is being brought to visit her today. She quickly gathers some biscuits and Diwali chivda she had secreted away and limps to the Gate. Only to come back in some time, furious as usual – 'That so-and-so sanstha lady didn't let me feed my child! I'll take her out of that bloody sanstha . . .' Reasoning with her is, of course, impossible. She's in her usual jerky state of permanent impotent rage.

Later, after I have been shifted to the Phansi Yard, I see her being released on bail. Thank heavens! In the short time I have been here, I have learnt that even the poorest, most destitute person in this jail prefers the freedom of her release to the security of these stone walls and the daily fare of bhatta doled out with a dollop of contempt.

11

Through the bars of the Phansi Yard, I spot this pair regularly walking on the jail path that goes around the rectangular ground: the shorter, bespectacled greying mother and her taller, plumper daughter in their green saris with their hair done up in braids, always deep in conversation. The unmarried daughter is a doctor, the widowed mother a lawyer. Often, they sit together reading the English newspaper that is allotted to their barrack. They don't do any chores – they are Brahmins, after all – and I discover they are not popular among their barrack-mates. Yet, disarmingly, both rush out with a blanket to catch a stray kitten that has got stranded on a tamarind tree. The daughter is particularly bouncy and rather childish.

They had been sentenced to death earlier and were then lodged in the Phansi Yard, in the two cells Shoma Di and I occupy, but the sentence has been commuted to life imprisonment, so now they are in the barracks. The story told about them is that a doctor had double-crossed them and had an affair with both mother and daughter simultaneously. They are accused of chopping him into bits and disposing of his body in packets in different places in the Western Ghats. The head has never been found. He was a married man and the complainants are his family members.

Once again I ask myself, what made them commit a crime of such vengeance – these competent, educated, independent women? Why was this person and his double-crossing so important to both of them that they could think of destroying their lives for vendetta? The mother fights her case herself. 'We will be released,' she claims confidently.

I wonder. The courts have been lenient with husbands who, having discovered their wives with lovers in a 'compromising' position' or even suspecting their wives to be unfaithful, have killed them or their lovers, or both, in a fit of murderous rage. This is because they have used the legal defence of the 'sudden and grave provocation' of discovering adultery. But with women it's a different matter. Perhaps they are not expected to have the emotion of rage at all?

Children

I enjoy looking through the bars at the children playing on the swings, the see-saw, the merry-go-round, and watching the young mothers bring their infants out in the sun.

Children are the freest human beings here. For these under-sixes the prison is a huge, relatively secure commune, full of women who have plenty of time on their hands to pet them and carry them, albeit in their rough-and-ready way. At the age of six, these children will be handed over to their families or to an institution.

One cute little girl is a particular favourite. She was born here and is gifted new frocks regularly, both officially, that is on festivals/birthdays, when something is bought from the jail budget, and unofficially, meaning clothes donated by the jail staff.

Another chubby infant is passed so often from hand to hand, by Constables and prisoners alike, I wonder if he gets tired of being kissed and pinched so often. Jail being an unpredictable place, excessive love for children can get you into trouble too. One day, while we wait at the Gate to be strip-searched before being taken to court, we see a junior staff member cuddling a baby boy. 'Hey, that's enough. He's the child of an accused after all . . .' a senior official admonishes her, scowling.

Caste, class and community hierarchies are at work here too, as elsewhere in the jail, though subtly. That talkative little one who lisps her 'grandmotherly talk' has a sour-faced mother who yanks her along as she cries. She gets little sympathy and not so many gifts, probably because she is the child of a Dalit mother.

The children here get a special diet. This includes, apart from the usual staple of small rotis, non-spicy aloo sabzi, khichdi and boiled eggs, occasionaly Parle-G biscuits and sometimes even Maggi noodles or til laddoos. All the children rush to the Gate to welcome the mamas (literally 'mother's brothers', but used here for male convicts) who haul in a cartful of rations and vegetables each day for the BC, because they all carry toffees in their pockets for the kids.

The kids inevitably pick up the rough jail lingo and the swear words that are commonly used. Like the adults, they call food bhatta and sleep bandi (the phrase for locking up), because they, like their mothers, are locked up in the barracks from 5 p.m. to 7 a.m., and also from 12 noon to 3 p.m. What will these children make of this life, I wonder, after they leave for a sanstha or are handed over to their families? How will they feel when they learn that in the 'outside' world all these beloved maushis (mother's sisters) whom they have been brought up by are considered criminals, and when the uniformed Bais (Constables) they meet outside cease to be affectionate as the ones in the jail?

Jail life, morally regimented and full of prying eyes, can sometimes be tough on children too. A little boy and a girl are spotted by a loud-voiced Bai while engaged in innocent sexual exploration behind the barracks. The boy is beaten severely by his mother. 'I was only taking her jhadti (search),' he protests, unaware of his 'sin'. The incident is the talk of the jail for weeks afterwards, accompanied by many 'ahs' and 'oohs'.

Only some children are lucky enough to have visitors from the world outside the jail. Those whose fathers and other male relatives are in the Main Jail get to meet them on the last Sunday of the month. They are carefully dressed up by their mothers with kajal and powder for this monthly mulakat. That is what 'family' means, when your parents are in jail.

Rules, rules, rules

The first thing one learns in jail is to obey rules. Rules that are not written or consistent, not necessarily legal, and sometimes not even rational. I realize this early when I see a woman Constable barking at an inmate in the lock-up, 'No clutchers in here.' In a few days here, I have learnt that this is only one item on a long list of things not allowed in jail – nail cutter, scissors, sewing needle, spoon, safety pin, empty plastic covers, hair clips, any fermented food (for fear it could lead to food poisoning), medicines not handed out from the Dispensary . . . anything that can be used as a weapon to harm oneself or others. I hear that in male jails, where corruption is rampant, powerful or wealthy prisoners seem to have access to all kinds of things, including drugs, mobile phones and special food, but to be fair I haven't seen much of this in the Women's Jail, apart from some slight preferential treatment.

Rules are implemented by a complex hierarchy. At the top are the Senior Madams, that is, the Jailer and her assistants; next the Head Constable and Constables – the Bais; below them the Warders, the Tais – convicts given supervisory roles for a wage of Rs 1,500 per month and distinguished by the yellow saris they wear. Then come the prisoners who do jail work on a daily wage and sometimes 'help out' informally. They also sneak on their fellow prisoners to the Tais/Bais in return for some privileges. These layers of surveillance sow divisions among the jailed, making each prisoner suspect the next. It needs only a tiny pebble thrown into a seemingly calm pond for ripples to be formed that reach far and wide. Why did A talk to B? What Canteen stuff did C pass on to D? E is wearing F's clothes!! For some time the whole jail becomes tense and rigid, and then, as the days pass, relaxes back into the human habits of mixing and joking and slyly transgressing the rules.

What makes the set-up wildly arbitrary, I realize after a few weeks at Yerawada, is that the rules change from Madam to Madam, Guard to Guard, Warder to Warder . . . 'Wear your dupatta when you come to the Gate.' 'Keep your chappals there.' 'Don't snore' (very difficult to obey, I found from personal experience). 'You can't read the barrack paper till the Warder Tai has.' 'Don't cross the garden of your barrack.' 'Who is gossiping over there?' 'Oh, so these steps [to the Stage] have been made for you ladies to sun yourselves on, have they? Get off them at once.' 'Don't talk to HER.' 'Don't dry your clothes there.'

But sometimes, when the women are gathered outside the barracks grumbling, arguing loudly and laughing raucously, and when they take their own sweet time to go back inside the barrack at lock-up time, one senses the unease, nervousness and anxiety in the voices of the staff trying to herd them in. Their instructions become louder and more frantic – 'Hey! You there! Go in quietly.' 'Stand in line.' 'Quiet there . . . quiet there.' Ultimately, the need for rules arises from fear – fear of the potential power of an unpredictable collective.

12

She's a young Muslim in her twenties, tall with a loud, manly voice, coloured rimmed spectacles and a long braid that she makes even longer with her parandi (tasselled hair ornament). Ever cheerful, she is a born manager and takes charge of Sunday cleaning operations in her barrack. And naturally, she takes the lead in organizing birthday surprises. Dressed in her colourful, even fashionable, salwar suits, she loves babysitting the chubby baby in her barrack before and after her Factory duties – for which she dons a smart white coat as her uniform. Irrepressible, she loudly sings snatches of film songs to him, her favourite being '*DJ wale babu mera gaana chala do*'.

She and her sister are facing trial in a kidnapping case. Rumour has it that she was not really involved, but her sister was. They are very different personalities who occasionally fight bitterly and are sent off to separate barracks. But they can't do without each other and are too dependent on each other to be apart for long, so after many requests in the Round, they are soon together again.

It seems the younger sister and her male friends had tried to extort money from a rich older man, using her (the younger sister) as a honeytrap. The old weasel turned out to be smarter than them and turned them over to the police, claiming they were trying to kidnap him. The older sister came to the police station to rescue the younger one and got implicated too. The two women are in jail for the last four years – they neither get bail, nor does their trial proceed – because the complainant refuses to answer summons and testify. The main accused – the leader of the group trying to extort money from the complainant – is apparently in 'negotiations with the complainant' and is absconding. It looks like the complainant has everything under his control.

The tragedy is, the older sister was doing an MBA and had a decent job in Delhi. Now her family has abandoned the two of them and don't want anything to do with these 'jailbirds'. Their brother visited them only once, to inform them of their mother's death.

Yet the older sister remains cheerful, despite these dire

circumstances. She is the 'choreographer' of the dances to be performed on 8 March, International Women's Day, and is the soul of the rehearsal sessions. But her sister reveals that she sometimes spends the whole night crying in the barrack.

She stops excitedly at our Phansi Yard. 'Hey, look at my drawing for the New Year, Aunty! "*Jail ke Sapne*"' (Dreams in jail). The drawing shows a caged bird in 2018, flying free in 2019. The last I heard of her, she was still in jail.

13

A new prisoner has arrived, obviously middle class, fair, with mousy hair in a 'messy bun', wearing steel-rimmed spectacles and platform heels. Accused of murder, she is given a green sari to wear, which she has wrapped untidily around herself and which looks very odd with her heels. On the first day she stands aloof, hesitating to mix, looking very lost. She is snapped at for not sitting in line for the Round, and for putting her shoes in the wrong place. She doesn't know Marathi either.

The next day a bright-eyed young undertrial in her colourful salwar suit calls her inside the barrack: 'Here, let me tie your sari properly.' And then another undertrial in a green sari befriends her, maybe to discuss her case, for this prisoner is a lawyer from Delhi.

The papers say she gave a supari (paid a hired assassin) to kill a man, but the shooters accidentally killed the guy's wife instead and injured a police sub-inspector.

I see the following morning that the children of the jail

have besieged her on the steps of the Stage chorusing 'Aunty, Aunty!' She is teaching them the alphabet, writing it on their slates to copy. In a day or two she has started yoga in a blue tracksuit given to her by the yoga instructor (another undertrial) and is haggling over accounts with someone she is paying to perform her barrack duties.

Like all of us, the world of women prisoners has assimilated her.

14

She's a thin, sharp-nosed young Muslim woman in her convict's green sari and hair in a bun held by a clutcher (some of the older or more privileged prisoners have smuggled these in and the Bais wink at it). You never find her walking leisurely. She is forever running between Barrack No. 3 in the Undertrial Compound and the Factory behind our Yard, or walking briskly, 'Indira Gandhi style'.

She is a 'watchman' at the agarbatti factory in the jail campus and brings dough, sticks and perfumed powder to our Yard for our neighbours – the death-row prisoners – to roll out agarbattis.

She is very bright and has a sharp tongue too, for which she is notorious. But she has a certain beauty when she smiles, which she does more often nowadays as she expects to be released in a couple of months.

Her son, nearly six and rarely seen with his mother, is as savvy as she is, though far sweeter and naughtier. He plays games with the bric-a-brac strewn around in the jail, leads the other kids in new adventures, generally has the run of the jail grounds and knows exactly which Bais to run away from at top speed. He tends to be made the scapegoat in every scrap involving other kids, and many of his mother's fights stem from accusations against him. She also beats him mercilessly.

Her sentence is coming to an end soon, but her husband, it is said, will be released later, and this has put a question mark on her release too. I learn with shock that if you are a woman prisoner without a respectable 'family' (read husband/father/brother) receiving you on your release, you may not be released at all but sent to a sanstha.

A woman is legally adult enough to be charged, tried and sentenced by herself but socially not adult enough to be released! Well, this young woman has decided that she is quite capable of looking after herself alone and is confident that she can find a way around the rules. 'I am going to Mumbai,' she declares.

15

The newspaper carries a news item that the twenty-eight-year-old in Barrack No. 1 has been sentenced to life imprisonment in a trial that took merely six months. She is a young woman who was in the lock-up with Shoma Di and is very quiet and hard-working.

She had a bad marital relationship, and one night, after a bitter fight with her husband, left him, taking her two infant children with her. She claims that she walked and walked and fainted on the banks of the Indrayani river. The allegation is that she drowned her two children. In other words, this is a case of double murder. The truth is probably that, like so many other desperate women in bad marriages, saddled with little babies, she tried to commit suicide by drowning herself and them. While she was rescued by a fisherman, the children died.

Yes, the death of the two children was a terrible tragedy and she bears the blame for that. But why are her young and overburdened shoulders carrying all the responsibility? The woman was abused and harassed by those very in-laws who are now accusing her of infanticide.

To add to her burden, her lawyer was appointed by the court on behalf of our failed legal aid system. How can she ever hope to be really 'heard' in any meaningful sense of the term?

16

The kinds of things that women can do for their lovers is frightening and pathetic at once.

One typically Punjabi beauty with long hair, thick eyebrows, fair complexion and sharp features is accused of poisoning her well-to-do family. Her parents and brother died.

Another woman is alleged to have cut down her mother-in-law with a sickle.

There is no family support for such women. No visitors, no money orders, often no lawyers of their choice.

A particularly tragic case is that of the tyrannical erstwhile Warder of the Hospital Barrack. An elderly woman, a stickler for discipline and cleanliness and an expert at distributing Canteen food (other people's, of course) to her various favourites, she was looking forward to her release. But the young lover for whom she killed her husband had been released several years earlier and has now made himself scarce. With no family to 'claim' her, we have heard that today she languishes in a sanstha, shorn even of her Warder status in the jail. It's a common story. Lovers often flee the sinking ship, just like the proverbial rats.

17

She is beautiful, with henna-coloured hair and large, expressive eyes, fair and tall. She has been sentenced to ten years' imprisonment for allegedly beating her disabled eleven-year-old son to death with a cricket bat. 'Culpable homicide not amounting to murder' is the legal verdict.

She had a vicious, abusive husband from whom she struggled to get a divorce. He was so cruel that the court had granted her custody of her son. She came to a new town and began her life afresh. She was living with a friend (or lover) in a rented home. Her ex-husband, who is the complainant, claims she killed the boy after he came upon his mother and her lover in a compromising position. But she says it was an accident that happened after she hit him in rage. She never intended to kill him. Though there is no evidence in the case, the aggressive lady prosecutor had insisted on a ten-year sentence.

Her ex-husband used to come drunk to 'visit' her in jail, only to mock and abuse her, and to threaten her with revenge. Finally, the jail barred him from visiting her as she would refuse to meet him.

She wants to appeal the verdict but is afraid her husband will contest it and may make things even worse for her.

Work

As I watch people through the bars, I realize how important work is to maintain one's sanity, purpose and rhythm in jail.

As the gates of the barracks open at 7 a.m., the work clock starts ticking. Women begin sweeping the paths and gardens of leaves, swabbing the corridors, each carrying out her allotted tasks.

The way women work, in jail and outside it, carrying out the hardest work for the longest hours and getting the least credit, angers one, but perhaps it is also the source of their immense shock-absorbing capacity.

Here, most of the convicts who don't get any money orders from home either work in the Factory, carry out jail work or work in the fields of the Open Jail.

Jail work means doing things like summoning the prisoners

(or rather shouting out for them) for mulakat or court; assisting the doctor, psychiatrist and social worker; keeping offices clean and filling drinking water for the jail staff; ringing the gong (called 'the Toll') at the appointed times of bandi and unlocking; stocking the Canteen; and handing out bedding and green saris. The distribution of letters and money orders is done by 'trusted' convict daily wagers who are paid only Rs 65 a day, but they are rewarded by becoming the privileged among the prisoners. They are also the 'eyes' and 'ears' of the jail administration. If the jail actually employed workers for all the tasks that these prisoners perform for little or no money, the State would have to dish out a pretty packet.

One of the most important tasks is cooking for the 350-odd women prisoners. Twelve or thirteen convicts who have worked earlier in the Factory and are known to be diligent are selected for this paid work, working under a Warder. They have to report early, at 5a.m. (even when the temperature drops to 7 degrees Celsius) and they work up to 5 p.m., when the prisoners are locked in. Cleaning and chopping vegetables, cleaning rice and dal, kneading dough and rolling out chapattis, cooking the vegetables, boiling milk, making tea, washing the enormous cooking utensils, filling water for kitchen use, taking breakfast to the barracks, tea to the staff, and bhatta to the Phansi Yard ... Their tasks are endless.

In each barrack, different prisoners are allotted, by rotation, the task of collecting the bhatta for their barracks for all meals except breakfast.

Some fifty or sixty convicted women go to the Open Jail every day between 8 a.m. and 4 p.m. and for half a day optionally on Sundays and holidays. They work in the rice fields and vegetable farms of the jail and eat their lunch-time bhatta right there in the fields. These farms supply the tomatoes, bhindi, radish, cabbage, pumpkin, beans, capsicum and various kinds of bhaji (green leafy vegetables) that we eat in the jail. We are rarely fed the better-quality rice that is grown in the fields of the jail. That crop is probably sold.

The women who work in the Open Jail are paid nominally, Rs 50 a day, but more importantly, each day of work counts as a day's remission in their sentence. Only women who have completed five to seven years of their sentence are physically fit, and whose behaviour is certified to be 'good' are selected by a Jail Committee for this work. (In the fifteen months I was in Yerawada Jail, we saw this committee hold court only once.) These are usually poorer, rural women, for whom the legal system is for all practical purposes out of reach, and ultimately they have to rely on the only thing they have – their labour – for an early release. Work in the Open Jail is tough and is carried out in all seasons – winter, summer or monsoon.

Work in the Factory is of five types – agarbatti-rolling, which is the most common, lowest paid, piece-rated work; the more skilled work of stitching at the sewing machines; the work of weaving strips of pattis, done by very few women who traditionally do this work; the work of making envelopes and preparing dasti pads (cardboard pads with flaps in which papers are tied together) for jail use, which is generally light work reserved for elderly women; and finally work on the extruding machines making automotive lock-set parts, which is given to smarter, younger and educated prisoners, who strut about in their white coats and caps. This work is carried out for a company called Spark Minda and is referred to by all as 'Minda work'. It carries on from 7.30 a.m. to 4 p.m., with a gap of an hour from 11 a.m. to 12 p.m. for eating bhatta.

The jails of the state of Maharashtra (and maybe even the country) are integrated through their prison industry. Rice, wheat, vegetables, soap, tooth powder, dhurries, sheets, files, furniture – almost all the jails' requirements are produced by prisoners themselves or by those of other jails. The system works almost like a network of vast State-run barter communes – on pitiful wages. Besides, the prisoners also craft objects of great beauty – pottery, furniture, candles, idols, carvings – that earn jails a good sum. The Jail Museum in Raipur is famous for the bell-metal sculpture of Bastar, mostly created by the indigent Adivasi prisoners of Jagdalpur Jail.

Exploitative though our system is, I am grateful that we have escaped the fate of prisoners in the United States where corporate entities sponsor prison industries. This has created a vested interest in long and harsh sentences, because what can produce more profit than a non-unionizable 'docile and disciplined' workforce of prisoners. Needless to say, America's prison population contains a disproportionately high number of poor black males.

Back in Yerawada, I find it interesting that the highest-paid monthly-rated workers are the kundawalis or sanitation workers – three or four of them – who get Rs 1,800 per month. A couple of decades back there were no toilets in the cells of the Phansi Yard but only earthen pots called kundas, and the kundawalis were actually manual scavengers disposing of human excreta. There is no longer any manual disposal of excreta in Yerawada, but the name kundawali has stuck. The current crop of kundawalis are not always Dalit; there are also women from denotified tribes and various backward castes. They work continuously from 7 a.m. to 5 p.m. (up to 3 p.m. on Sundays) cleaning toilets, swabbing the common corridors, clearing waste, bathing the disabled prisoners, washing the mats and bedding of the staff, helping the Public Works Department (PWD) clean drains and carry out minor repairs, carrying furniture from place to place and generally doing every possible odd job, including climbing the roof to sweep off autumn leaves, disposing of a dead cat or rat, or scouring the utensils in which chicken is brought from the Main Jail, which the other BC workers won't touch because they think it's a dirty job to clean them.

I too want to work. About three months after I came here, I moved an application to be permitted to use my skill and experience to help with the legal aid work in the jail. As I expected, my request was rejected.

(I was not to know then that I would be inundated with this work in the future, given to me not by the jail but by prisoners, when we were transferred to Byculla.)

Friendship

We are strangers here, thrown together by force of circumstances and made to sleep, eat and work side by side. We are women of different regions, socio-economic backgrounds, castes and temperaments. These create divisions, yet friendships are formed, and it is these friendships that are the key to one's survival in jail.

It is touching to see women clapping at the news that someone has got bail, to see them embracing thrice, in the manner of a Muslim greeting, when they part, to watch them caring for each other's children, for someone ill or pregnant, and quietly looking after newcomers.

But maintaining such friendships is a delicate art. The moment friendship becomes solidarity, that is, if a prisoner publicly stands up for another, the jail administration steps in to stamp it out. 'Why are you interfering?' 'What do you have to do with this?' jail officials ask brusquely, making loyalty sound like a criminal offence.

A young lawyer who began protesting about how undertrials in Barracks 3 and 4 (in the Undertrial Compound) were discriminated against vis-à-vis convicts in Barracks 1 and 2 (in the Convict Compound) was punished by transfer to another jail. People tell me this as a warning when I want to help with cases that seem badly stuck.

The biggest crime of all, of course, is women loving each other. The slightest suspicion of a lesbian relationship leads to instant separation, invites sexist abuse from the jail staff and provides plenty of juicy gossip for everyone else. It's only after I understood the deep phobia, rather horror, of lesbianism felt by the jail authorities that I was able to figure out why no one is allowed to wear 'manly' clothes here, such as T-shirts, jeans, trackpants, etc., and is forced to wear either a sari or a

Punjabi suit WITH A DUPATTA. Yoga clothes are the only exception, and that too, a recent one.

And yet, in the interstices of such repression, I see the inmates' tolerance shine through. A prisoner from Gujarat has a beard and a moustache, a manly face, and refers to himself as a man. However, he has a woman's body, menstruates and has to wear a sari or salwar-kurta. Aside from the fact that he lives in a women's jail and wears women's clothes, he seems to have an absolutely normal life here and is accepted far more unconditionally than he might be in the outside world. He sits in the sun with a wad of tobacco in his cheek, tenderly looking after a month-old baby while the child's mother goes about her chores. He has been here eighteen years now and is keen on a hysterectomy because he sometimes bleeds twice or thrice a month. His likhaan (record of sentence) has already come and it's a matter of a couple of months for his release now. And indeed, while I am still at Yerawada, all of us watch him leave the Gate in a smart checked shirt and dark trousers.

Religion

I've discovered only one culture is officially allowed in jail – religion. So, we have Brahma Kumaris coming to preach each morning, for which ten or twelve, mostly elderly convicts, gather at the Stage. On Thursdays, a Christian lady comes to lead songs in praise of Jesus. Sometimes there is a ten-day course conducted by the Art of Living folks, which draws educated middle-class women. It begins with feel-good exercises and ends on the last day with bhajans.

Even the musical programmes in jail are mostly around festivals and bhajans. Ganesh Chaturthi is observed with great fanfare, and an idol is installed in the factory shed of the jail, where some young boy child (once even a three-month-old) presides as chief priest!

Diwali means rangolis drawn outside the barracks, Chinese lanterns hung on doorways and the buying of chivda, besan ka laddoo and karanji (what north Indians call gujiya) from one's Prisoners Personal Cash (PPC) account in jail.

Not just Muslim, many Hindu women too fast before the festival of Eid.

At Christmas we were able to buy sponge cakes and cupcakes baked in the bakery of the Main Jail. Like all non-vegetarians, we ordered chicken too, which is served only five times a year in Yerawada – for both Eid festivals, the day after Dussehra, and for Christmas and Easter.

Several times in the weeks before and after Christmas, various Christian organizations come to give a performance or pray and sing carols, though mostly stressing that 'believing in Jesus is the only way to reach heaven'. ('*Darr ka bijness,*' as the Bollywood character PK in the film of that name would put it.) But the entire jail looks forward to these visits because the Christian organizations distribute warm clothing, cupcakes and soaps to all the children.

There are about twenty Christians, most of whom turned to Christianity after entering jail, and they gather on

Christmas morning to sing 'Hallelujah' among themselves in a corner of the garden.

Interestingly, the prisoners have their own pragmatic version of secularism. 'No harm in praying to any God if He [of course, how could God be a She?] gets me released!' So, we all eat our Christmas cake as devoutly as our Diwali puranpolis and our sheer qurma on Eid.

When I look around at those who attend prayers and sermons regularly, one can see that in the helpless and sometimes hopeless situations that they are in – a legal system they cannot comprehend, a society that has more or less cast them out – perhaps just 'having faith', 'remaining calm' and 'relying on Him to do miracles' are their only options. As Marx said, you indeed need some 'opium' to survive this 'vale of tears'.

On 1 January, jail staff and prisoners awake to a freezing morning (it was 7 degrees Celsius the previous night) and prisoners wish each other with a heartfelt *Lavkar sutun jawa* (May you be released soon). This is the one common greeting on all festivals.

18

She's a short, old Bhil woman, about sixty-five, with white hair and a big, red vertical line of kumkum on her wrinkled forehead, wearing her green sari in the typical Bhil fashion, just below her knees and with a long pallu wrapped around and covering her head. She came to this jail four years ago, after being lodged as an undertrial in another jail. She was convicted of murdering someone who was found dead in her field. She speaks in a childlike sing-song mix of Marathi and Hindi and probably her own Bhilala language. Most people here think she is 'simple' or maybe just a little mentally backward, and quite incapable of the premeditated murder of which she has been accused.

One day, when she is given two bright saris by a visitor, she excitedly asks someone's advice – which one to wear for Diwali? (On festivals, even the green-saried convicts are allowed to wear colourful clothes.)

She moves around alone, but follows the ebbs and flows of the barrack. She's always one of the first to rush to the water tap to fill her water bottles when the barracks are unlocked at 3 p.m. after the 12–3 afternoon bandi. She also sits obediently to hear the Brahma Kumaris every morning and religiously receives prasad, even though she seems not to understand or participate in the talk.

She's most animated looking after kittens, to whom she gives her share of the morning milk, and they purr their love in her lap. Occasionally, she sits alone in the sun with her empty aluminium plate and bowl after finishing her meal, looking far away into the distance. Where does she transport herself? To her home, her village, her forest? If only there was a magic carpet ... Then she has to be roused. 'Eh buddhi!! [Hey old woman!] Didn't you hear the Toll?' She laughs at herself apologetically and runs bow-leggedly back to her barrack.

Before we left Yerawada, she was released. Possibly, her children decided to appeal and her sentence was suspended by the high court. That day she waited a long time at the Gate, carrying, apart from other things, a small bucket somebody had given her to use. The social worker who was to accompany her was late, so she was once again locked in the barrack. She refused to come out later that evening, when the social worker finally arrived with tickets for the overnight bus, but finally relented and went off with her. A few days later the social worker told us how the two of them had to walk for several hours to reach the village where her small, bare hut stood.

Fights

As Shoma Di puts it, 'Fights are a way of life here.'

And what else can one expect? Put fifty or sixty women in a barrack, a lot of them tough cookies, many of them sharp-tongued and frustrated and some of them weepy and depressed. All sleeping on contiguous strips of the stone floor, disturbed by each other's snores, children, nightmares and trips to the loo. Forever accusing each other of stealing chappals, biscuits, 'better' green saris, 'better' utensils. Always arguing furiously over whose turn it is to sweep or swab or bring bhatta or empty the waste. Each forming her own peer group of region, language, community or 'type of case' (for example, there is the NDPS group, all charged under the Narcotic Drugs and Psychotropic Substances Act) to grumble together and abuse others. So, fights are bound to be a regular phenomenon. Usually, these consist of yelling and abusing, and the Constables quickly intervene to quieten down the combatants, who go back to their respective camps for a post-mortem and to plan the next stratagem.

But on one occasion, in the middle of the night, a physical fight breaks out in a barrack in the Undertrial Compound after lock-up, leading to loud shouts and wails, audible even to us. We stand at the bars of our cells and watch as the Constables rush into action. Phone calls are made to the Senior Jailer Madam and the Jail Doctor. The main contestants are dragged to the office near the Gate, arguing all the while. Fortunately, there are no serious injuries and the doctor leaves after examining them in the Dispensary. The barrack concerned is given a collective dressing down and the Constables watching it are put on extra alert. The jail quietens down.

But now the postscript: The next day, just before lock-up at 5 p.m., a wholesale transfer of fifty-odd women from Barrack No. 4 to Barrack No. 2 and vice versa takes place. This is standard punishment, carried out every now and then. Women holding their rolled bedding, aluminium utensils, water bottles, bundles of clothing of all shapes and sizes and dragging along reluctant kids move in both directions in two straggly lines between the two compounds. The announcement, as always, is sudden. Prisoners can only curse under their breath. Within half an hour the migration is over. No questions asked. This is jail. New barrack, new adjustments, new neighbours, new grievances, new fights . . . 'After all, tomorrow is another day' (with apologies to Scarlett O'Hara).

Food

The meal timings at the jail needed a little getting used to. Imagine collecting your dinner at 3 p.m. on a Sunday and then being locked up until 7 a.m. the next morning. This means storing food to eat later and keeping it safe from ants and cockroaches, and for us in the Phansi Yard, from cats and rats too. This is a skill all prisoners learn quickly out of necessity. They also learn how precious plastic carry bags, plastic tubs (particularly those with lids) and pieces of string are.

After hearing of the terrible quality of food in the Chhattisgarh jails and sampling the food in the Faraskhana lock-up, where you would have had to be a deep-sea diver to locate a piece of vegetable in the watery gravy, the Women's Jail in Yerawada is a pleasant surprise. In the Phansi Yard, or even in the Hospital Barrack, quantity is never an issue, because there are not that many prisoners to share the food with. However, food deemed tasty can become scarce in the larger Undertrial Barracks consisting of sixty to seventy prisoners each.

We get three chapattis, a reasonable quantity of rice, a decent quantity of a seasonal or green leafy vegetable (methi, shepu, palak, choulai, rajgira) and sufficient dal (moong, masur, arhar, matar and chana) for two meals. These are at 11 a.m. and 4 p.m., except on Sundays when dinner is at 2.30 p.m.). Breakfast is poha, upma or suji ka halwa and (diluted) milk. Tea is served twice a day (at 7 a.m with breakfast and at 3 p.m.).

We also get a few tomatoes, onions and, occasionally, even

radishes and raw sweet potatoes as salads, and three or four bananas a week.

(Food at Yerawada, we realized when we were in Byculla, was better than at other jails because (a) the jail was right next to the open fields where many convicts went to work and, more often than not, the vegetables were from these fields, and (b) because it was a team of women who did the cooking.)

Usually, jails have different varieties of 'food corruption'. One method common in Chhattisgarh is to have a parallel kitchen run by the long-term convicts, for which charges are extorted from the families of the prisoners. Another one, also common in Chhattisgarh, is the siphoning off of the goodies sent to jail by relatives of the inmates.

Here, in the Women's Jail at Yerawada, these primitive methods have been more or less eliminated by a Canteen system which I think is worth emulating in other states. This is how it works: money can be sent to a prisoner by money order, at present the maximum limit is Rs 3,500 per month. (It was increased to Rs 4,500 by the time I left.) This money is deposited in their PPC accounts, and amounts for the Canteen are deducted every first and fifteenth of the month on their instructions. This money can be used for purchasing soaps, shampoo, toothpaste and oil; buckets and mugs; envelopes, notebooks, paper, pens and stamps, and other necessities. It can also be used for buying a variety of biscuits, sev, peanuts, jaggery, sugar, jam, pickles, murmura and, interestingly, even tobacco. This has killed the most thriving jail black market of all – that of tobacco.

Of course, this is where class enters the picture. So, the

haves of the jail are those who get generous money orders and the have-nots are those who don't or whose jail wages are too meagre for purchase of most of the Canteen items. The haves can therefore contract out their jail duties of physical work in the barracks – sweeping paths, swabbing floors, watering plants, bringing bhatta, etc. – to the have-nots in return for the Canteen items they purchase for them, notably tobacco for the addicts. Even their own personal physical tasks – washing jail bedding, washing clothes, filling buckets for bathing, etc. – can be farmed out. Of course, there are long arguments over the hisaab (accounts) and the rates of various jobs, but the eternal rule prevails – if one doesn't have capital, one always pays for goodies through lots of labour.

If one has money in one's PPC, then one can also buy seasonal fruits (oranges, papaya, apples, guava, anaar, chikoo) from time to time, sweets and snacks at festivals, and a daily supply of eggs (at that time somewhat overpriced at Rs 6 each), of which meticulous records are maintained. There are no eggs in the months when there are many Hindu religious fasts.

Of course, over time, and despite all these embellishments, the tastelessness of mass cooking and the not-so-healthy oils used get to you, and chronic stomach complaints are only too common.

All the same, longings do not cease. Over time, I learnt that to satisfy those longings, women had devised the most ingenious of recipes. Here are a few samples:

Recipe 1 – Bhelpuri: Take murmura and mix it with the oil of pickle (both available in the Canteen). If and when you get tomatoes and onions (as we occasionally did in Yerawada), cut them with the edge of your aluminium katori (no knives, remember?). Mix with sev from the Canteen.

Recipe 2 – Laddoos: Take peanuts and crush them in your katori using the cap end of a water bottle filled with water for weight. Crush jaggery the same way. (Both peanuts and jaggery are available in the Canteen.) Mix the crunchy and gooey mixtures and roll them into balls.

Recipe 3 – Dahiwada: First borrow some dahi ka jaman (curd starter) from a co-prisoner and set the raw milk one can buy in the jail to make curd. (Remember, dahi or any other fermented food is forbidden, so this is a clandestine activity.) Take two pavs off someone on a special medical diet (many are only too ready to 'sell' their pav for some Canteen goodies). Soak them in the dahi. If the fruit on the tamarind tree outside your Yard is ripe, surreptitiously stone some down. Crush ripe tamarind in sugar water to make a chutney. Sprinkle sev on top of the dahiwada and serve with tamarind chutney!

19

She was short with bobbed hair, and strode along in tomboyish style (and to hell with the dupatta!), belonging to a relatively better-off and more Hinduized Adivasi family which had migrated to the city. She was accused of radicalizing youth to join the Maoists. In the four years she had been here, she had been acquitted in three of four cases registered in the tribal Gadchiroli district in Maharashtra. These trials were mostly conducted through videoconferencing, and the trial of the fourth had just begun when we entered.

Suffering from congenital heart disease, and consequently from serious breathing difficulties, she had had several operations and was still on a whole lot of life-saving drugs. One day, as we waited in the lock-up of the district court before being taken to our respective courts, she said with simple and unaffected bravery, 'Well, whatever one has left of life, one lives it fully!'

For the first twenty-five months, she was in a cell in the Phansi Yard and was permitted in the corridor of the Yard for only two hours because of the nature of her case. On top of that, the death-row sisters were encouraged to make her life very difficult. She was hospitalized many times and finally moved to a general barrack only when she fell into a breathless faint after mosquito repellent was sprayed behind her cell.

When we saw her she was on a special, salt-less, boiled food diet which the women working in the BC gladly provided, because she lived in Barrack No. 1 as they did and was popular and helpful, particularly in writing applications for the illiterate women amongst them.

Of course, all prisoners in political cases were solemnly warned not to speak to her, and vice versa. And no wonder, for the rebel in her was irrepressible. One day, in the 'Big Round' after Diwali (when the senior officers of the Main Jail all marched in for inspection), she was ready with samples of not-so-good chivda and karanji to show the Superintendent, and to ask whether they were worth the hard-won meagre wages of the women. She was, of course, the only one to speak up, though privately everyone was delighted. And obviously, this irritated the Senior Jailer Madam, who reacted by withdrawing any little relaxation in the rules they had allowed her earlier (like the exchanging of books or Canteen goodies when she went to meet her husband in the Main Jail). Once, during an Art of Living course, after nine days of yoga and pranayama, when on the last day they began singing 'Hare Rama Hare Krishna' bhajans, she stormed out, grumbling loudly, 'Pah! Finally the same nonsense religion stuff.' She was a voracious reader, had read everything in the library and could be seen each morning returning the previous day's newspaper allotted to her barrack to the office, no doubt after reading it from cover to cover.

Her family had disowned her after she married a Dalit co-activist. His family members, on the other hand, though extremely poor, were very supportive of both of them. Every last Sunday of the month she would wear a nicely washed salwar-kurta and dupatta to go and meet her husband in the Main Jail. Her current demand, which the Inspector General of Prisons had apparently conceded during his inspection several months back, was to make such family visits fortnightly, like in other jails. Truly she was one of the Brave New World.

(When we were in Byculla, we heard of her death. When we left she was already ill and weak, and her stomach had bloated like that of a pregnant woman while her arms and legs had become like thin sticks. Her application for bail had been rejected by the sessions court and was pending in the high court. It seems that she was taken for emergency neurosurgery by the jail authorities without

*informing her husband or seeking his consent, even though he was
lodged just across the road in the Main Jail. She did not survive
the procedure.)*

20

It's her voice singing Tukaram abhangs (devotional folk
songs) in a loud, powerful voice, floating down from Barrack
No. 2 to our Phansi Yard that wakes us up in the cold January
mornings after the six-o-clock Toll. She is the Warder there
and tries to wake up her sixty-odd 'wards' before the morning
Total at 6.30 a.m. With her mehndi-coloured hair, her long
red tika, and her weather-beaten face wrapped in the pallu
of her yellow Warder sari, she is a familiar sight all over the
jail as she walks briskly around. Try as she might, she comes
across as more motherly than authoritative. When she tries to
settle fights, she goes off into her own fast-paced emotional
monologue in a rural dialect that is difficult to understand;
and finally the Bais have to calm her down as well. She is also
unlettered, like a large proportion of the women here, which
means all the tasks of making the frequent lists – of Canteen
deductions twice a month or orders for the occasional special
food item – have to be done by the younger, smarter and
literate girls in the barrack. But she is universally loved and
respected for her unstinting labour in every jail task. She is
truly a jack of all trades. Be it constructing a cement step,
digging a flower bed, brushing the autumn leaves off the
tiled roof of the barrack, or trimming the branches of an old

tree, she tucks up her sari and is on the job. It is difficult to believe that this woman had cancer and has been cured after undergoing chemotherapy during her jail sentence, which has lasted more than a decade now. A cheerful soul, when she sits in the winter sun to distribute bananas or tomatoes and onions to the Barrack No. 2 inmates (notorious for their quarrels), she tries to be fair and deft at once, and dissolves potential arguments into laughter with her imitation of fruit-sellers – '*Kela lo, kela lo!*' (Bananas, bananas!) She comes from a family of kirtankaris (devotional singers), though she is equally happy singing hymns in praise of Yesu (Jesus), something she learnt in jail. When I hear her sing '*High court ke kone kone mein, mere Yesu ka thikana hai! Supreme Court ke kone kone mein mere Yesu ka thikana hai . . .*' (Jesus is everywhere, in the high court, in the Supreme Court), as a lawyer I feel a pang of guilt for the simple faith that people continue to have, their hope that they will get justice . . . which they never might. And we in the legal system are just not doing enough about it.

21

The saddest sight is of the very old prisoners. I am thinking of an old Brahmin lady from UP, tall and fair with snow-white hair, big, round eyes and buck teeth, who is at least eighty years old. The rules say that once a woman prisoner given a life sentence has completed fourteen years and reached the age of sixty, she is entitled to be released. This woman may not have completed the minimum term of her sentence, yet the jail administration is trying to procure her release because she seems to be suffering from dementia. No one from her family visits her. It seems that six or seven years ago, a son had helped her get a few days of parole. She left happily, thinking she had got bail. But it turned out that this was only done to have her transfer her share of property and land to her children. She came back weeping. After that her son visited her only once.

I see her deteriorate before my eyes. When I had just arrived at Yerawada, she would slowly hobble up with her plate and bowl to collect her bhatta or bring her water bottles to the water tap to fill drinking water. She would make her way to the raised platform when the Brahma Kumaris came to preach in the mornings and would sit there patiently, hands folded in a namaste, and collect her prasad. It even seemed that she was reading their handouts, though how anyone her age could do that without spectacles was beyond me. But one day I saw the Warder of her barrack half-holding, half-dragging her to the Hospital Barrack, another prisoner following with a vessel of hot water to bathe her. The irritated Warder was mumbling, 'Just this morning we bathed her, she has no control over her motions, she has soiled her sari . . . She doesn't remember she has already had her bhatta and comes to take it again.'

I hear she was very supercilious when she first arrived. She wouldn't touch Canteen food and wouldn't accept anything from the hands of a lower-caste person . . . Now all that is history, she is just another helpless old woman. Of late, as she hobbles slowly past our Phansi Yard, she has developed a strange habit. If my eyes meet hers she gives me a laborious namaste. I return it sheepishly. She evidently thinks I am one of the Bais. Each day I think, tomorrow I will not look at her. It seems so false to delude her about my identity. But it feels mean to deprive her of that tiny bit of recognition and dignity in her condition.

I can well imagine her being a tyrannical mother-in-law. Perhaps she did kill or at least drive to death her daughter-in-law, as many other incarcerated women have? Even so, what purpose is served in keeping her in jail now? As she says philosophically one day, gesturing towards the sky as she passes by the bars of our Yard, *'Oopar bhi jagah nahin, aur neeche bhi jagah nahin!!'* (No place for me in heaven or on earth!!) A couple of months down the line, we do see her being carried out of the Gate, virtually on her deathbed, on a ghongri held by four prisoners. Finally, her release order has come. Her family has come to collect her. The prisoners in the Hospital Barrack tell the Constable on guard at the Phansi Yard: 'Madam, do you know, we were waking her up every three hours last night, just to make sure she stayed alive. It would have been so terrible na, if she died without being able to go home!'

Mango Days

Finally the freezing cold is receding. The sunless Phansi Yard, nicknamed 'Kashmir', is the coldest place in the jail. Shoma Di and I have spent the nights huddled in our two blankets (each of us was bestowed a second one, thanks to our being senior citizens) trying to protect ourselves from the cold air floating in through the open bars. I find it helps – a little – to lie down in the left corner of my cell along the wall where there are no bars. There is no question of covering the bars (we must be visible at all times to the Guard) though some of the nicer Constables do allow you to do that briefly with your chaddar when you are bathing at the back of the cell or changing your clothes.

I have now mastered the art of bathing in a tiny space in the Indian-style toilet, crouching awkwardly behind the waist-high 'wall' that separates the toilet from the rest of the cell and spreading out one leg at a time. One has to perform these contortions to avoid being seen through the bars. Things are worse for Shoma Di, who suffers from a painful condition of arthritic knees. After a long legal battle, she succeeds in getting a plastic chair to use in the daytime between 9.30 a.m. and 5 p.m.

Duties of the Constables at the Phansi Yard change every

week. Gradually, our relationship with them begins to soften around the edges. We begin to sympathize with these young rural women, mostly living away from their families and coping in tough working conditions. There are conversations about in-laws, husbands, further studies . . .

Our neighbours, the two sisters, have frightening mood swings. Suddenly they turn jealous and accuse us of 'becoming more friendly with the Constables', or claim that we get 'more tea' when the convict working in the BC brings in our breakfast and that we 'laugh and gesture at her'. They tell tales to the Superintendent. One day the elder sister even tries to threaten Shoma Di, lunging at her. Fortunately that day, we have a very strong Constable on duty and all four of us are promptly locked back into our cells. We are relieved when a day passes with no palpable tension in the air.

As the summer advances, water troubles begin. The taps in our cells have dried up. Now we need to buy buckets from the Canteen and are let out of our cells to get water from a communal tap – four buckets for all purposes, and four bottles of drinking water. To-ing and fro-ing from the tap to the cell, a five-minute walk away, is especially painful for Shoma Di, who can only carry half buckets because of her arthritis. During every Weekly Round by the Jail Superintendent and assorted officials, we raise this problem, but everything moves so slowly . . .

Yet something historic has happened. As the hot weather approaches, first our male co-accused in the Yerawada Main Jail and then we, in the Women's Jail, put in requests for fans in our cells. Our neighbours, as always, are sceptical. 'They will never allow it in the Phansi Yard. We have not had a fan for more than twenty years. Someone might use it to commit suicide,' they scoff.

(Actually, that is physically impossible, since the ceilings of the cells are too high.) And believe it or not, a few months down the line the request has actually been accepted. Of course, the actual process of fitting the fans is strewn with red tape. The staff from the PWD has to be present, as does the jail electrician, and they have to be accompanied by women Guards. And special permission is needed to get the tall ladder out of the Hospital Barrack. The fans arrive two by two – of course our neighbours will want theirs fitted first. Finally, all four fans have been fitted – ancient ones brought from the Main Jail godaam (godown) where they have been rusting for some time. My fan makes an awful racket – squeaking, creaking and whirring – and to watch the long stem wobble is very scary. Even the Guards peeping in to see what the noise is about are worried that it might fall. Anyway, I use it only when it's really hot in the afternoon or the mosquitoes are unbearable. Like the lights in the cell (which are on at all times) the fans can only be turned off and on from a board located outside the cell at the end of the corridor. That means you have to stand at the bars of your cell and request the Guard on duty to do it. Yet it's a breath of fresh air . . . literally.

Mango Wars

What would we have done without the beautiful old trees in Yerawada Jail? The old banyan in front of the Hospital; and the younger one just beginning to send its aerial roots down, and under which someone has established a Shivling, which stands near the Toll gong; the neem tree at the gate of the

Phansi Yard; the tamarind trees in front of the Activities Hall and behind the solar heater; and of course, the mango trees – five or six of them – in the open ground in front of us. Each day the ground is full of leaves of all shapes and sizes and beautiful hues, some of which I collect during our half-hour walk, to press under the hefty chargesheet filed against me by the Pune police in umpteen spiral-bound volumes that stands in a corner of my cell. I sometimes send these pressed leaves to my daughter in lieu of a greeting card.

As the mango season approaches, we watch the flowering and then the small green unripe kairis (raw mangoes) appearing in clumps on the mango trees. They grow bigger and riper, and then begin the Mango Wars. They start with a few bolder prisoners taking potshots with sticks and stones at the kairis, ignoring the shouting and scolding from the Constables. But as the mangoes ripen further, going from green to orange-yellow, they begin plopping down. Sometimes parakeets and crows try to peck at them and make them fall. In these heady times, when the gates of the barracks open at 7 a.m., only half the prisoners rush to the toilets and bathhouses. The rest run straight to the trees to pick up mangoes that have fallen during the night, to sort the sweet from the sour, and whole ones from the half eaten. The first to rush towards them are the children, and I am surprised that they don't get cricks in their necks as they desperately crane them upward. I notice that each barrack has its little team of expert stone/stick throwers, egged on by the others, and each zealously guards the trees nearest to them.

Around noon every day, a whole flock of green parakeets

arrives to nibble at the fruits and, interestingly, rather than being frightened by the groups of women gathered round the trees, they seem to enjoy playing to the gallery and pushing the fruits down. '*Padla, padla . . .*' (It has fallen . . .), the cry goes out, and all the women clamber over each other in their eagerness to get hold of a ripe mango. One day, as we are out for our airing, a mango obligingly plops down in front of me. It turns out to be soft and ripe, a lovely sweet-and-sour one. In the night, a kindly Constable who has found some more, rolls a mango under the bars and winks at me, 'Have it.' In jail, you begin to pay attention to all the things you usually take for granted. You notice trees, birds and animals, you connect with the sights and sounds of the changing seasons, and you begin feeling grateful for those things. So, like everyone else, I am affected by the mango epidemic.

22

She's our in-house 'heroine', this plump and pretty undertrial. She has acted in a few Marathi TV serials and videos and has quite a filmi aura about her. Given to talking dramatically, reciting poetry, shaking a leg to catchy songs, teaching others how to apply cream ('in circular motion'), and calling a baby in the barrack 'sweetheart', she likes to believe that rules are for lesser mortals and that she is an exception. Of course, she greatly dramatizes the events of her own life.

It seems she was cheated by a producer and perhaps even sexually abused. 'I gave it back to him,' she says. Another case of #MeToo but not one to keep silent for fear of losing out on work, she apparently broke into his house and assaulted him. She has now been accused by him of stealing Rs 6,000. Surprisingly, she hasn't got bail though it's nearly a year now. According to her, it's because her case is being tried by a MCOCA court (the Maharashtra Control of Organised Crime Act has stringent bail conditions) and there have been endless adjournments. But is she actually charged under this draconian law? Even she doesn't seem to know.

No one could call her despondent. Though not very tuneful, she sings a popular naughty Marathi song, with a karaoke track in the 8 March International Women's Day programme. Later she claims that the male jail staff could not keep their eyes off her.

'Oh heroine, go inside, didn't you hear the Toll?!' the Bai shouts at lock-up time, as she continues to comb her long hair in the corridor even after the bell rings. (That's another rule – you are not allowed to comb your hair inside the barrack.) She flashes a cheeky smile and goes into the barrack.

23

She is strong and well built, with a smile as bright as her nose ring lighting up her lovely dark face. She is a kundewali, a jail sanitation worker. Ironically, this caste-determined work that Dalit and some OBC prisoners take on and no upper-caste prisoner would ever volunteer for, is the steadiest wage work that jail can offer. The Bais call her 'black beauty', but not in as unkind a way as the nickname suggests. She hails from the Vadar community, one of the denotified 'criminal tribes' of the colonial era. Her imprisonment began four years ago. From 7 a.m. till 6.30 p.m., she is allowed to stay outside the barrack even after the bandi to complete her work. She has a long string of duties that include cleaning the toilets, clearing the waste, swabbing the corridors, bathing the old and disabled, washing the bedding of the night-shift Bais and assisting the safai karmis who come to unchoke the drains. Apart from all that, she is generally at the beck and call of everybody. You can hear her name being shouted from all corners of our jail ... 'Hey, get me a bottle of water,' 'Bring the registers to the Gate,' 'Come and throw some water on this cement, otherwise it won't set,' 'Get the tables and chairs for the programme,' 'Bring the long bamboo from the store to clean the cobwebs in the BC.' Despite all the running around she does, she is usually pleasant, though occasionally, indignities like being talked to in a tone only reserved for 'people like her' bring a flash into her eyes. But when she is happy she giggles and skips around like a child, and only then does one remember how young she is.

Of late she is more confident, as she has found a younger co-worker, a plump, strong and cheerful assistant, and you find them oiling and combing each other's hair and eating together, the signs of close friendship in jail. Even out of her meagre wages (Rs 1,800 a month) she sends money home to her mother and her younger brother, an eighteen-year-old with a wife and kids.

Her story is typical. Married off at a young age to an

inveterate drunkard, she bore his daily beatings with fortitude, till one day she retaliated, and weak as he was, it killed him. She says her mother-in-law didn't say much against her in court, but some of her husband's relatives and community elders did. Her lawyer was a novice allotted by the legal aid department. It was his first case under Section 302, and she has been sentenced to life imprisonment. Being illiterate, she doesn't know if any appeal has been filed.

Since her marriage was part of an arrangement of satha-lota, common in her community – a brother and sister marrying another sister and brother – her nanad (husband's sister) is also her bhabhi (brother's wife). After the murder, her bhabhi has cut off relations with her natal family and continues to live with her brother. But her own daughter – now thirteen years of age – is with her mother-in law. On a recent visit, her sister told her that her in-laws don't send her daughter to school and make her do lots of housework, so she has fixed up a marriage for her. When we express shock she says, 'Well, I won't send her off (to her husband's house) so soon, but in our community, we all get married early. I was married too by that age.' She wanted to get parole leave to attend the marriage, but couldn't. Meanwhile, the fate of another 'black beauty' – her daughter – hangs in the balance. Will it be better than her mother's?

Legal aid

Of all the disappointments of jail, perhaps the greatest, for me as a lawyer, is the condition and quality of legal aid. Many of the convicted women do not get money orders and their wages are too modest for them to afford competent lawyers. Some of them do not have visitors, and even if they do, their families are not in a position to engage good lawyers. So convicted prisoners do not even seem to know the status of their appeals in the high court or Supreme Court – whether their case for a 'suspension of sentence' (pending a decision on an appeal) has been argued and decided, or even who their lawyers are. Nor do lawyers come to meet these clients or write regularly to them. During a trial, a prisoner is taken to court and has an opportunity to observe what is going on, baffling though the legal system may be, but the convicted are truly forgotten.

Time and again, I mull over how legal aid in the higher courts could be made more effective and meaningful for prisoners, and I have some thoughts.

Well, for one, all legal aid counsel up to the high court level, on being allocated a prisoner's case, should visit their clients in jail as soon as practicable and obtain detailed instructions in an effective conference, and this should be budgeted for by the Legal Services Authority (LSA). The complete record of the client's case must be made immediately available to the legal aid counsel at the LSA's expense. All legal aid counsel should seek instructions at least by telephone, if not in person, before every substantive hearing, and the jail should ensure such communication. The legal aid counsel should, without any delay, inform the client of any order passed by the court by post as well as by email to the Jail Superintendent, if not by personal visit.

Are you surprised that these seemingly basic aspects of a

lawyer's accountability to a client need to be talked about? Let me assure you that the legal aid lawyer's accountability, if there is any, is unfortunately only to the LSA and not to the prisoner. This is what needs to be changed urgently.

Over and above that, the prisoner's counsel should immediately be informed of any significant change in the prisoner's circumstances – ill health (both physical and mental), pregnancy, childbirth, situation of access to and custody of children, and new information regarding her case so that, with the consent of the prisoner, the proper applications can be moved. The legal aid lawyers attached to the jail should assist the prisoners proactively by communicating with their counsel, accessing their court dates and translating their court orders. There is so much fanfare about digitalization and the online uploading of case status and orders, but there is no appreciation of the Herculean efforts a prisoner has to make even to get to know her next date of hearing or what the last order was. The jail should promptly report to the LSA if a legal aid counsel is found negligent or indulging in unethical practices.

Even in the high court, as far as possible, the prisoner must be allowed to remain present in the court for final arguments, for consultation or instructions to her lawyer, and for queries of the court. This in itself could avoid miscarriage of justice.

I am aware that legal aid lawyers are very poorly paid, but then that needs to be changed. Ineffective representation is no representation at all, and so what if those represented are indigent prisoners. It is still human lives that are at stake. It's a heartbreaking situation.

24

After blaring headlines and demonic descriptions in the newspapers, one expected someone quite different. She and her brother-in-law were brought from Dubai, where they had fled to after the Bombay blasts of 1993. She claims they had been given an assurance of being made approvers. Her brother-in-law was executed in Nagpur Jail a few years ago, and she is serving a life sentence that will probably last her natural life. Apparently, a vehicle that was used in the blasts was registered in her name.

She is tall and stands upright even though she is quite elderly. Wearing the green salwar-kurta of a convict, she always has her head covered. Her sharp-featured face appears peaceful. We see her taking a walk along the jail paths alone every morning. She goes to the Factory to do sewing work in the daytime. She stitched 400 blouses last year, but says there was only enough cloth for 115 blouses this year. She's usually quiet, but smiles and exchanges pleasantries with her co-workers as they wait for the Factory gates to be opened. Since she gets regular money orders and other necessities, perhaps the work is mainly to keep herself occupied. She is intensely religious, doing her namaz regularly and keeping rozas during Ramzan. The sound of the azaan at nearby masjids is clearly audible here. For all the notoriety of her case, she is generally treated respectfully and is called Aapa (elder sister) in her barrack. Our society has a lot to learn from prisoners about acceptance and tolerance.

Correctional service?

Prisons are no longer called prisons; they are now called 'correctional services'. But the most important thing needed to make that change real – namely empathetic, socially sensitive, confidential and professional counselling for inmates – is missing. But it never seems to be missed by the jail administration.

What do these women prisoners feel about themselves, their spouses, their natal families, their children, their lovers . . . ? Perhaps they are sex workers, who usually return to the trade, but suppose they don't, can they survive? What was the context in which they committed their 'crime'? How far do they think they were responsible for what happened? What role did they personally play, and how do they see their role?

What do they need to begin life afresh? Education? Training? Psychiatric treatment? Financial assistance? Looking at the women around me, I see that looking after children, working to fill up their days or for pocket expenses, and friendships formed amidst this adversity are the only things that sustain them at present . . . and they are not enough to assure them a future once they are released.

Health

What the Women's Jail at Yerawada does have is an extremely kind and responsible woman officer in charge of the Dispensary. Patients of TB, HIV, diabetes, hypertension, are all regularly provided medicines, sometimes quite expensive ones. Patients with TB, HIV, other kinds of debilitating diseases, lactating mothers and pregnant ones, and some of the very old women are recommended special diets. This consists of pav (bread), two eggs and a packet of milk each day, or peanuts and jaggery for the vegetarians, provided twice a month. Each week, on different days, a gynaecologist, a skin specialist, an eye specialist, a dentist and a paediatrician sit in the Dispensary, and one of the Tais goes around shouting in the barracks and the Factory . . . '*Skinche doctor aale e e e*' (The skin doctor is here), '*Dantache doctor aale e e*' (The dentist is here), as the case may be. This is, of course, apart from the regular Jail Doctor and psychiatrist. Psychiatric medicines are doled out at night to each patient, who obviously cannot be trusted to keep the medicines in their possession. The women Constables do this on their Night Round, shouting at each barrack gate: '*E goliwale, goli khane aao*' (Come and get your pills).

The referral hospital for Yerawada Jail is Sassoon Hospital. Like every other government hospital, it looks overcrowded and bewildering at first glance. But at closer quarters, it is reasonably efficient and has competent staff in most specializations. The jail more or less ensures that prisoners who are referred there are taken to Sassoon periodically in batches, and also in emergencies, including childbirth, even in the middle of the night. Infants are taken there, too, for immunization.

Children under three are routinely shown to the paediatrician when he/she visits the jail, whether their mothers ask for it or not.

All in all, there may not be the luxury of a 'bedside manner', but there is a basic framework in place for primary and even secondary healthcare. (We have prisoners here recuperating from cancer and bypass surgeries.) This, together with a special diet, means that women who come from deprived socio-economic backgrounds from rural areas, and their children, have a better chance of being scientifically treated here than at home. It is a tragedy and an irony that they have had to come to jail to obtain their right to health and that we have not been able to provide this to our free citizens in the last seventy years. It is an equally great irony that despite this, if you ask the sickest woman here whether she prefers treatment to being released, she will choose freedom.

(Later, after being transferred to Byculla, I realized that Yerawada, being a central jail, and also because it has a large proportion of convicts who are long-term residents of the jail, has better financed and systematized medical facilities than most of the district jails. The miserable experience of prisoners during the pandemic exposed all the deep fault lines of medical care in prisons like Byculla, but more on that later.)

25

Today, we saw our first andolankari (agitationist) prisoners: Four middle-aged lower-middle-class women – one older and unable to walk very well, another apparently a Muslim woman from her salwar-kurta and absence of a bindi – all wearing sweaters and shawls, and in an easy relationship with each other. It seems that they were protesting against their houses being demolished for the widening of a highway. They had gone to protest at the corporation's office (must have been a gherao, in which they surrounded officials) and were booked under Section 153 IPC (preventing a government servant from carrying out his duty), which has been made a non-bailable offence recently. These women must be local leaders of sorts. It feels good to see that they are not nervous or weepy, but come and join their barrack inmates with their jail bedding and aluminium vessels in hand and try to learn how to go about living here. Where to get food and to throw waste, where to bathe and dry clothes . . . Two of the more agile ones do the swabbing of the corridors of their barrack, as their share of barrack duty. They have been arrested on a Friday to ensure that they spend Saturday and Sunday in jail, a common ploy by vindictive police officers bent on 'teaching agitators a lesson'. On Monday evening they are released after bail orders are passed by the concerned court. We watch them leave their barrack with their beddings and jholas (bags) when their names are called out from the Gate, just after the bandi. 'Hey, where are your vessels?' shouts the Senior Bai from our Phansi Yard, as she supervises our being locked up for the night. 'They have food in them, Madam . . .' they reply. But they are allowed to leave, even though the rule is that those leaving the jail need to return their vessels. In a women's jail, there is at least an unspoken consensus that food shouldn't be wasted. The vessels can be returned to the utensil store the next morning.

Education

Teacher Madam is a laid-back, uninspired and uninspiring lady who walks slowly around the jail like a tortoise. That perhaps explains the sad state of the 'library' – a grand word to describe a small steel almirah with two rows of Marathi books and one each of Hindi and English books. The handful of books in greatest demand – pulp romantic novels, mainly in Marathi – are always issued out, while the religious stuff usually remains on the shelves. After having read all the English books available there, mostly donated by the British Council, from a dog-eared copy of *Rebecca* by Daphne du Maurier down to (sorry, fans!) the Harry Potter books, I am finally offered a copy of *Majhi Janmathep* (My Life Sentence) by V.D. Savarkar in Marathi, of which there are, not surprisingly, multiple copies. I actually plod successfully through half of it, learning Marathi as I go along.

The first part of the book is absorbing for its vivid description of extremely tough prison conditions at the Cellular Jail in the Andamans, where Savarkar was lodged as a political prisoner. (The latter part, with its anti-Muslim slant, provides less incentive to plough on.) I feel like telling Teacher Madam that the book describes how the political prisoners fought with the British jail officials for a library and succeeded in creating one, which finally had four to five thousand books, including classic authors like Plato, Lenin, Mills, Tolstoy, Tagore and Garibaldi. Meanwhile, I still haven't managed to get the five books that my lawyers are trying to send me, despite having an order of the court in my favour.

Sometime in May, Teacher Madam supervises the handful of prisoners giving exams in the Hall. It appears that this is through the Yashwant Rao Chavan Open University Programme. The credit for this should go to the prisoners, however, since we never see Teacher Madam encourage or assist anyone to study. Despite the lack of any guidance, I am impressed to find that our elderly Warder, who heads the BC, is sitting for her 'fifteenth' class exam (i.e., BA final year) this year, having cleared her fourteenth class last year, though she finds it a little difficult to remember in which subjects!

26

I see her from the Yard, sitting on the Stage when the Brahma Kumaris have their morning preaching sessions, but she sits apart from all the others, and not on a chatai (mat) like them, but on the floor. I see the 'devotees' gesture to the Mata (the woman preaching), wrinkling up their noses as if to say 'she is not nice', 'we don't like her', and 'don't give her prasad'. While the Mata admonishes them, she makes no move to include her in her sermon. I wonder about this prisoner's psychological state. Was it the cause of her 'crime'? Or its product?

This woman, with a limp, a snub nose and a mass of wiry grey hair, is always alone. Right now she seems to be reasonably clean and neatly dressed, but she must have been in a far worse shape earlier, physically and mentally, for all the Bais speak about her not bathing for days and how during the weekly jhadtis of the barracks, her stuff would be full of rotten leftover food and stinking clothes. Now she is one of the many

71

who have a goli at night (psychiatric medication). The Bais make sure she comes with her water bottle to the locked bars of the barrack and swallows the pill right in front of them.

A few months earlier, she had got violent with a Warder during the afternoon bandi. She wanted to go and have a bath, and obviously the Warder couldn't let her. Several Warders and Bais had to rush to the barrack to keep her in control. When I was into my fourth month here, I had heard her raised voice outside the barrack for the first time, as she scolded someone in fairly decent Hindi. 'Hey, why did you take my rotis,' she said. 'I feel hungry at night. I am a human being, after all!' It was a relief to know that she could defend herself, but she probably imagines persecution where there might be none. A couple of nights later another 'episode' occurs. Someone makes a nasty comment about her when she goes to fill water at the common tap. She begins shouting and cursing steadily and loudly about how everyone ill-treats her. Even after being shepherded into the barrack at bandi time, her tirade doesn't cease. The Lady Jailer arrives to assist the dozen Constables gathered outside the bars. After half an hour of alternately being soothed and scolded, she calms down. It's so clear that many women here need psychotherapy, not punishment.

27

On another day, as the Brahma Kumaris' Om Shanti pravachan (sermon) is going on the Stage in front of our Phansi Yard, we hear a voice confidently piping up and telling the preacher, 'Oh no, Mata! We are very blessed here. Just think – not having to cook, only washing one's own clothes and vessels. No husband to order us around. No mother-in-law to nag us if we nap in the afternoon. No stream of guests to feed and serve endless cups of tea to ...!' What a wonderful description of the worldly prison called patriarchy and, just think, she had to come to a jail to escape it.

She is a thin woman with delicate, typically Maharashtrian features. Dressed in her white Minda coat over the green sari of the murder-case undertrial, she works in the Factory and attends the pravachan whenever possible. Beneath her audacity, she has her anxieties. She is also an HIV patient.

She was living with her husband and three small children and used to run a small shop. Her landlord's elderly father used to come to collect the rent and perhaps was friendly with her. He was, however, having constant fights with his son. One day, when she met him at the hospital, she says he asked her to keep a small pishvi (cloth bag) for him at her shop. She heard after a couple of days that he had been found dead. On checking the bag, she says she was shocked to find that it contained some family jewellery and surrendered it to the police. The old man's son went on to accuse her of murder, and a huge crowd surrounded her house and abused her. Despite there being no direct evidence of her involvement in the old man's death, her bail has been rejected by both the lower court and the high court. Even assuming that the story is not as simple as her narration makes it out to be and that the old man had perhaps been enamoured of her ... a murder charge? It seems a little far-fetched. She is worried about her bail application, which has now been filed in the Supreme Court.

She sings and acts well, and has been included in a play the Om Shanti team is putting up for the International Women's Day programme. Ironically, the philosophy of the play seems to be diametrically opposite to her own spontaneous comment. Its message is along the lines of 'All that we suffer is because of the sins of our past lives. And if you are a woman, you must have been a very oppressive man in an earlier life.' In other words, carry on – doing good and feeling bad.

28

In the dark of the court lock-up she looks so young, with her bright eyes, silky braid and colourful synthetic sari that we are all shocked to learn that she has a twenty-four-year-old daughter and is, in fact, a grandmother twice over. In her lively way, she relates the hilarious and sweet story of her child marriage. She was only thirteen when she was married off to a twenty-year-old, who lived a few lanes away from her maternal home. For the first year, she used to run straight back home at night to her parents and complain to them, 'He keeps on wanting to touch me!' After a day or two, her parents would diplomatically persuade her to go back. The surprising part is the patience shown by her husband and in-laws. Gradually, she says, she became fond of her husband. Once her mother-in-law conspired to leave the two of them alone at home, and he went off to sleep on a separate bed. It was she who snuggled up to him and asked him to hold her. And then there was no looking back. She says with obvious pride, 'He helps me in everything – the children, the kitchen, the shopping, the cleaning . . .' He comes to meet her in jail and is supportive. She says wistfully, 'Yes, I made a mistake, but won't the court understand that I didn't mean to?' It turns out that she and her friend, also in Yerawada, are charged with murder and kidnapping.

This is a pattern that repeats itself. A prisoner shares a slice of her life in a way that is very relatable . . . and then comes the dark story of which the contours are not clear. How does one respond? It is a dilemma. The way I resolve it is that I'm not going to sit in judgement on her. She is suffering enough.

To return to the story, there is also a third co-accused, younger and a little aloof. This third young woman is fasting, is not wearing chappals for her court appearance, and indicates, through gestures, that she has taken a vow of silence. To impress the court, I wonder, or to avoid answering questions? When she returns to the lock-up after the hearing, she starts speaking and says, 'Our two male co-accused who are innocent should be let off . . .'

Later, I become aware that the situation is even more complicated. This third woman was in a vulnerable state and had been sheltered by the other two. All three appear to have been implicated in a case of kidnapping of a child and murder of the child's mother. But the third girl has now turned approver in a case where there doesn't seem to be much evidence. Of late, she has been bragging publicly about how she will soon be set free. She studiously avoids her former friends in the jail premises, and though they travel together in the same police bus and sit in the same lock-up, they don't speak with one another. In jail there is not much sympathy for such approvers, who are looked upon as backstabbers and touts of the police. In the men's jail there might have been a physical attack on someone like that. One prisoner hints darkly, 'What does she think? That she will get away with this? "They" will surely get her outside.'

Women's Day

International Women's Day, which falls on 8 March, is officially celebrated at the Yerawada Women's Jail sometime during that month with a two-hour cultural programme. Prisoners show off their talents before senior jail officials, including the Director General of Prisons (who happens to be at the present time a woman). Very good performances can occasionally lead to a couple of months of remission in sentence. There are no speeches or talks, let alone debates and discussions, around women's rights or laws relating to women. No one is going to be discussing patriarchy here, or the long struggle that women have waged and still wage for equality. Still, the very observing of 8 March does generate enthusiasm and a feeling of freedom.

Preparations begin in February. Senior Jailer Madam puts a few talented (and trusted) prisoners in charge of selecting women to perform five or six short dances, a few skits and a couple of songs, each item lasting a maximum of five minutes. Eventually, some forty women are chosen, with a bit of favouritism thrown in. Most are convicts, since they are long-term residents of the jail, but this time some talented longer-term undertrials have also been included. These women are allowed to rehearse during the 12–3 p.m. bandi when the rest are locked up, and on Sundays and in the final days of preparation, even for half an hour after 5 p.m.

So, for a whole month we hear dance music and dialogues all around us. NGOs are asked to pitch in with costumes, fake jewellery and make-up, which turn out to be of quite a professional standard. Male prisoners from the Main Jail come in to fix the pandal, and professional sound technicians are called in. Finally, when the great day dawns, I can see, from the back window of my cell, the performers dressing up and being made up in the Factory. An accommodating Bai takes photos with her cell phone (which she is, only for this programme, allowed to bring into the jail) while everyone jostles around her pleading, 'Take mine too, with my friend ...' They will be given prints of these pictures later – perhaps the only happy souvenir of many years of lost youth.

Even we, the denizens of the Phansi Yard, are taken to see the programme and seated on the floor right at the front of the prisoners' side of the pandal. In the other half of the pandal, rows of chairs have been placed for jail officials, families of Constables, NGO people. The first row consists of sofas for the chief guests. Lest anyone should forget for a moment that this is happening in a jail, twenty women Constables are lined up all along our side of the pandal, holding batons of moulded plastic. These are trainee Constables who have no doubt been told that we prisoners are a dangerous lot.

After a long wait, during which kids and kittens

wander all over the Stage, provoking both amusement and admonition, it becomes clear that DG Madam won't be coming, and the programme begins with the Yerawada Jail Superintendent presiding. It's like watching a family function because one knows all the participants. Two young women dressed up as male comperes do the introductions. The dances are very good and the skits turn out better than their rehearsals. The kiddies' dance is a hit and the child of a Senior Jailer Madam wanders on to the Stage to join the prisoners' children. The programme ends with the inevitable 'Jhingaat', a wild dance number from the now cult Marathi film *Sairat*. (Isn't it extraordinary that this song has become so popular, even as the caste atrocity at the heart of it – a brutal honour killing over an inter-caste marriage – is never discussed?) We hear later that even the prisoners and Bais sitting at the back of the pandal got up to dance to 'Jhingaat'. We can't see them because we are obediently facing stagewards, mindful of the batons. Our Jailer Madam gives a speech about how the performers prepared all this by themselves 'without any disturbance to their Factory or work schedules'. The Superintendent gives a speech promising some remissions even though DG Madam couldn't come because of a last-moment engagement. The participants take a bow and deliver some emotional and distinctly overdone praise for the officials. And it's over . . .

Before the make-up is removed and the participants are locked in, at the UNIMAGINABLY late hour of 7 p.m., there is another spontaneous performance of 'Jhingaat' in the maidan. The day has come . . . and gone. And even if not acknowledged properly, and even if celebrated under the shadow of batons, it has brought a whiff of freedom.

(In Byculla, an undertrial jail with a high turnover, 8 March is not such an elaborate affair but, conversely, it is much freer and more spontaneous, organized by whoever among the prisoners is in favour at the time, and attended by only Byculla Jail officials. On our first 8 March there, a mere fortnight after our arrival, Professor Shoma Sen makes a short, thought-provoking and moving speech about the origins of 8 March. The year after, I am asked to speak about legal aid, and a group of youngsters, including Jyoti Jagtap, also jailed in the Bhima Koregaon case, put up a hard-hitting skit on patriarchy, which brings tears even to the eyes of the women Constables!)

29

Recently, at the tap while filling drinking water, this young woman shared her relief that she had started her MC (jail lingo for menstrual cycle). She has changed over the past three or four months that she has been here, filling out physically, looking more relaxed and beating her cute toddler son less. She was worried about not getting her periods for the past five months. But now, like a truant child, she aims at the green mangoes and rushes to gather them, cheered by her barrack-mates on the veranda and cursed by the Bais.

Her husband is a long-distance truck driver. He and two of his friends, a truck driver and helper, are imprisoned in the

Main Jail. It appears he and his friends were drinking at their house. The other two had just had an altercation with the truck owner, who was later found dead. All four of them – the three men and she – have been arrested for murder. She claims that she and her husband are innocent and only made the mistake of sheltering the other two. It's not an implausible story; it's not unknown for poor employees to be made scapegoats in the high-profile murders of their employers.

She's a very hard worker and takes part in all the barrack and garden work – carrying tins of water on her head to fill the hauz (tank) in the common bathing shed, carrying tins of soil to make a flower bed, or wielding a broom to clean the paths of leaves in the morning. She has little patience with her son, whom we call '*bina brake ki gaadi*' (brakeless vehicle). Once he starts walking, Newton's First Law takes over and he finds it difficult to stop, leading to several accidents. Recently, he almost ran off the Stage into mid-air and was caught just in the nick of time. She is tired of running behind him and tries to curb his enthusiasm harshly, leading to loud wails. Fortunately, he has adopted another indulgent old prisoner as his 'grandmother', who generally enjoys the task of playing with him and teasing him while his mother is busy.

One day I see his mother crying. It turns out her mother-in-law had come to visit, and only as the old lady left the mulakat window did the prisoner notice her older, seven-year-old son hidden under the pallu of her mother-in-law's sari. She had not even been able to speak to the child over the mulakat telephone. She had rushed to complain to the Senior Madam at the Gate, who was luckily one of the more sensitive and helpful ones. The Madam shouted out at once to the old woman and called the little boy into the Gate and let his mother give him a hug. She sobs, 'My mother-in-law says, "Give the little one to me too." Then what if she doesn't let me meet him either? My reputation is ruined . . . I'm a jailbird now.'

30

Two 'co-wives' are among us – the second wife younger, taller and fairer, better educated and articulate, and the elder obviously a rural wife, short and quiet. Their husband, an investor who owns several companies, TV channels and even newspapers, is charged with financial fraud related to the Saradha chit fund scandal. This has led to multiple lawsuits across several states and agencies. The wives were directors, though what exactly they knew about their husband's business is not very clear.

The second wife has been in jail for close to two years now and was probably the one living with him in the city. She has been taken to different jails all over the country and speaks in a knowledgeable way, comparing Yerawada Jail to Bhubaneswar and Visakhapatnam jails. 'In Bhubaneswar, our relatives could bring us food,' she says. (Yes, that would be important for the better-off prisoners.) 'But Visakhapatnam Jail is the most free,' she continues. 'The Naxal prisoners have got many improvements made there.' The elder wife had absconded for about nine months after the offence was registered. She describes how she moved constantly from place to place with a small stove, a small cooker, a couple of utensils, a shawl and a change of clothes in a couple of jholas – quite captivating, this story of the long-suffering wife as an underground fugitive. The two of them seem friendly enough and are always together. They can be seen devoutly praying every day at the Om Shanti sermons. Hopefully not for ending up with the same husband in their next seven lives.

31

A painfully thin girl, she is dressed sometimes in a green salwar-kurta and sometimes in a green sari. She has large, expressive eyes. She had an affair with a married man and has been arrested for the murder of his wife. The man and two of his friends are incarcerated in the Main Jail. Our male co-accused, who are also in that jail, had heard them talking among themselves in the lock-up about putting the entire blame for the murder on her. When we tell her this, she says, 'But I love him.' She works in the Factory and looks after children in the barrack. She dresses carefully on court dates. One feels like warning her, 'Hope you have a lawyer of your own, don't trust the men's lawyer blindly!' But as they say – love is indeed blind.

32

Nowadays she has court almost every other day, this smiling woman in her late thirties, dressed in smart churidar-kurtas and a loose ponytail. She is the one who had taken me under her wing on my first day at the Hospital Barrack. All her five cases have reached the stage of the Section 313 statement (when the accused is given an opportunity to reply to all the incriminating circumstances listed out by the judge). 'We will give two lakhs to the public prosecutor,' she whispers to us in the lock-up. She, her husband and her then juvenile son, now eighteen years old and out on bail, have been charged with extortion and criminal intimidation under MCOCA. 'It is all political,' she says, showing her husband's card which bears the name of an obscure party and photographs of many Dalit Bahujan icons. It is one of many groups which have become a blend of militancy and goondaism, a systemic reaction to systemic social injustice and inequality.

She has been here for a couple of years now. She had a hard time initially, when her sister – entrusted with the task of sending money orders to jail – chickened out. And then she contracted or was finally diagnosed with TB. When I first entered the Hospital Barrack she used to wear a mask, which actually accentuated her large, beautiful eyes and made her look younger. She was friendly and helpful and told me all the dos and don'ts, particularly about not asking anyone about their case, the thing that came most naturally to me as a lawyer. Her younger sons are with her family. She is confident that she and her husband will be released by and by. 'My husband says he wants a daughter now,' she says, with a bashful but proud smile. She is worried because her husband has been on a hunger strike in the Main Jail against not being taken to court, and unlettered herself, is dictating a six-page love letter for him to her friend.

33

She's been convicted with a life sentence for pushing her mother-in-law off the terrace when they were drying clothes. She is slim, pleasant-looking and efficient in her work. It's a bit difficult to imagine her as a murderer, and one wonders what might have been the provocation. Yes, they do say that she does not tolerate any nonsense and has a violent temper, though she seems to keep it on leash most of the time. She is the watchman of the Minda Factory and we see her, in her smart white coat on top of the convict's green salwar-kurta, walking purposefully to the Gate twice a day with the records of output and attendance.

She's part of a threesome of young prisoners, and the fourth who joins them often is a slightly older Warder. They sit together at lunch – sharing, teasing each other, arguing, grumbling, giggling . . . Being quite popular with the Madams, she has got a fifteen day parole, and one of her group-mates, an otherwise cheerful young woman with a loud voice, is in tears. But a few days later, this friend excitedly tells one of the Constables on duty in our Yard, 'She phoned my family and asked after all of them . . . they told me so in the mulakat!' Love can only be shown in little gestures here, and how precious they are.

34

She's a strong, well-built woman with a crescent-moon vermilion mark on her forehead, full of confidence and grit.

She is different, in the way political prisoners often are; they don't come with a burden of guilt, they retain their dignity and encourage others to pluck up courage. She introduces herself as a karyakarta of the Bhim Army. She and their Maharashtra president were picked up while putting up posters the night before the visit of their party leader Chandrashekhar Azad 'Ravan' on 31 December 2018. Surprisingly, they were charged under Section 153 IPC (obstructing a public servant from performing his duty). How? When they neither obstructed nor resisted anybody? They had been refused anticipatory bail even by the high court. Finally, they surrendered in court. Despite the offence being so trivial – due to its obvious political nature and because they had surrendered – the judge is refusing them bail. She attributes this to the manuwadi (casteist) politics of the BJP government here in Maharashtra. She describes with pride how, when Chandrashekhar finally visited the village of Bhima Koregaon, which has an important place in Dalit history, an hour's drive took him nearly six hours because he was mobbed by so many young admirers who wanted to shake him by the hand.

She's in Barrack No. 3 in the Undertrial Compound, where she advises her barrack-mates and tells them to keep their chins up and fight. 'I would have liked to be a lawyer,' she says wistfully, 'but I chose to stop my studies and become a karyakarta instead. After all, even that work is important . . .' I agree wholeheartedly . . . perhaps it is more important.

35

She was released yesterday – this tall, broad woman with a sweet face and a curly black ponytail – acquitted after four years plus a wait of two months for the judgment. Her story, like the story of so many others here, is not black and white but full of greys. She married her childhood sweetheart, a Dalit man. Her well-to-do Punjabi family wasn't happy, but bought them a flat. She was working with Infosys in a temporary job. Over time, she claims, her husband's drinking and abusiveness became too much for her. By that time, her elder daughter was seven and her younger daughter two years old. She walked out on her husband, filed for divorce and started staying with her mother.

She says her husband had taken a loan from a goonda moneylender and had an altercation with that goonda two years after she left him. The goonda has even apparently confessed that he has killed her husband. Yet, on her mother-in-law's complaint, she, her sister and brother-in-law have all been accused of arranging a contract killing. Her pregnant sister gave birth while in jail and eventually got bail. She claims her mother-in-law has political connections, and so has been opposing her bail tooth and nail. She says she has left the flat for her mother-in-law. Her own children are with her mother.

It's possible that there were serious conflicts over property and money. Also, there is gossip in the jail that her family was rich enough to 'manage' the court. It seems like a bittersweet story, with love, hatred, caste and class all playing complex and uncertain parts. But as she stands at the Gate with her two bags, waiting to leave, many friends hugging her, wishing her good luck, all one can feel is a sense of immense relief . . . at least one more prisoner has gone home.

Overcrowding

The board at the Gate of the jail says, 'Official Capacity – 129'. But all the time I have been here, the numbers have fluctuated between 250 and 350.

There are four main barracks, two each in two different compounds separated by a big, solid iron gate. One compound is for convicts and one for undertrials. The Convict Compound, which contains Barracks 1 and 2, the Hospital Barrack, the Phansi Yard, the Factory, BC, the bathing houses, toilets, a playground for the children and the solar heater, is relatively spacious, and the jail opens directly into it. The Undertrial Compound also has bathing houses and toilets, apart from Barracks 3 and 4, and the Library (if indeed it deserves such a grand name) is housed there. You enter it through the Convict Compound. It is relatively small, yet two more barracks are being built there!

In Barracks 1 and 2 there are mostly convicts in their green saris or green salwar-kurtas, and a few of the long-standing undertrials. Barrack No. 4, though in the Undertrial Compound, houses mostly those convicts who have undergone more than seven years of sentence and who go to work every day in the Open Jail or in the rice and vegetable fields adjacent to the campus of the Women's Jail. Barrack No. 3 is the undertrial barrack with a floating population – the most crowded and colourful.

Generally, the barracks house sixty to seventy prisoners. However, when they were being painted, one by one, the inmates of the barrack which was being painted would have to be 'adjusted' in other barracks. Then there were at least ninety to a barrack and no one could sleep.

In the ordinary course, each prisoner has a narrow strip of floor to spread her bedding and sleep on and a small space at the head of it, to keep her jail utensils and a bag of clothes. The spaces along the two longer walls are most coveted, for then you have a wall to sit against and a permanent place to keep your bags. For those who are unfortunate enough to have to sleep in the middle of the barrack, their clothes have to be neatly rolled up in the bedding and their drinking water bottles and utensils placed beside them in rows during the day.

Obviously, there are huge fights over space. One can barely turn over without disturbing someone else. And then there is the steady commotion of children crying and the TV (allowed till 9.30 or 10 p.m., depending on the strictness of the Bais on duty).

Each barrack has one bathroom and one toilet, and since inmates are locked in from about 5.30 p.m. to 7 a.m., the rule is to use the toilet only for urinating as far as possible, and to take turns to fill the common drums of water to keep it clean. The queues for 'No. 1' (urination) begin in the barracks at around 4.30 a.m. In Barrack No. 4 (where prisoners work in the fields from 8 a.m. onwards) the line starts as early as

2.30 a.m. When the barracks are unlocked at 7 a.m., there is a mad rush for the toilets (six in each compound), and mind you, one has to fill and carry water there too. In the bathhouses, most women dip their buckets into the common tank – a hauz – and bathe in the central portion of the bathhouse, which has a drain along its length. Those seeking a bit more privacy, like the older women, carry water in their buckets to cubicles with half-doors. Someone puts it well: in jail there are lines for everything – to piss, to shit, to get food, to cut your nails, to see the doctor, to have a mulakat . . .

The Hospital Barrack has an 'examination room' and two other rooms, but two out of three of them are used to store green saris, brooms, beddings and bundles of the extra clothes that prisoners are asked to put away. (Prisoners are only allowed to keep two sets of clothes with them and at the most a 'better one' for court.) There are mostly old women and invalids in the Hospital Barrack, and just a few younger ones who go to collect the bhatta and help take care of the women who can't manage the daily tasks themselves. They all sleep in the barred and locked veranda at night, and routinely, in every Saturday Round by the Superintendent, demand fans. Like us, they are lucky this summer – their fans have arrived.

Isolation

Our Yard, the Phansi Yard, now more benignly called Separate Yard, was once called Karanti (probably the colloquialization of 'quarantine'). We spend long hours locked up in our single cells.

For someone like me, notorious for making a virtue of not looking after myself, isolation has meant not having an excuse for doing that. So I actually do the exercises I never had time for before, eat regularly and take my medicines for diabetes and depression. Since there is no scope for any snacking, and barely any sweets, my sugar is more or less under control. Having mastered the art of bathing at the back of the Indian toilet, I actually start having the most unhurried baths of my life. In comparison with the barracks, here we have the luxury of 'a single cell with attached bathroom', and 'room service' to boot.

Of course, the nights are long and can be taken over by reflection or swamped by anxiety, depending on one's temperament and state of mind. Night-time in a single cell is a nightmare for the hypochondriac, a little bit of whom we all have within us. Are my arthritic joints more swollen today? Is that a varicose vein? A new patch of eczema? Aches become more painful, mosquitoes buzz louder and sleep evades one. One makes friends with the strange shapes in the plaster. Stone walls painted over, as they are here, create many such shapes, which start looking to me like faces or animals. I am reminded of the eerie story 'Face on the Wall', by Edward Lucas, which I had read as a child, in which the narrator describes a face he 'sees' in the patches on a wall, which begins to dominate his entire existence.

It is during the nights that the kittens come into our cells to play. We have four of them – all of the same litter – brought up by the two sisters who are our neighbours. One of them has taken a fancy to me. She comes in, mews insistently to be given a place on my lap, lies down luxuriously to get her neck stroked, plays around in mock hunting poses with my pen or book or newspaper, and finally curls up to sleep next to me. True to my personality (I find it very hard to say no to anyone) I let her bully me . . . and enjoy it.

It is in the night that I do my writing. Writing letters to my daughter. Writing notes about other prisoners. Working on a book I am translating. Writing notes from newspapers. And reading whatever books I have. And of course, reading the voluminous chargesheet. And then there are all the Sudokus I have carefully torn out of the newspapers Shoma Di and I subscribe to. (We have to return them next morning.) Even at home I have problems with sleep, but here they have gotten worse. More often than not, when the Constables and sometimes the Jailer or Assistant Jailer herself, come on their late Night Round, I am still awake reading or writing. 'Go to sleep, Sudha,' they say, not without concern.

Yerawada Jail is so full of trees that we hear bird calls of many kinds in the early morning before the bandi opens. One bird, which I haven't seen, I have christened 'the doorbell bird'. I had never imagined that that very irritating doorbell sound that you sometimes hear when bells are rung in people's homes actually existed in nature.

Fortunately for us, our isolation is not complete. There is a lot that we can see through our bars. We may be kept 'separate' but we are still very much part of this strange, many-coloured creature called the Women's Jail.

36

The thin, sour-faced woman with a deformity in one eye came into the jail when her youngest daughter was just five days old. Her story: her husband, an abusive alcoholic, had been demanding sex just after she returned from the delivery, and when she refused, he insisted that she send her elder daughter, aged eight, to him. That was why she killed him, she says.

The little daughter she brought with her is around four now. After many months we see the woman today, in her 'civilian' clothes, being taken to the Baramati court where her trial is still pending. Her elder daughter, who lives with her dadi (paternal grandmother) is to testify at the next hearing, she tells her barrack-mates when she returns. She never seems to have any visitors, nor does any lawyer come for a legal interview. She goes to the agarbatti factory every day, making Rs 300–400 a month rolling out agarbattis for six hours each day, enough to get her little girl biscuits from the Canteen. The daughter loves to 'help her' by filling the water bottles and generally doing errands of the fetching and carrying kind. She has a cute lisp, but is a bit of a crybaby, constantly running to her mother with loud complaints, often exaggerated, that other children are bullying her. Her mother has little energy and patience for her, but straddles her on her hip and continues doing whatever she was doing before. The Constables accuse her of 'not looking after her daughter', but I think, looking at her taut, bitter face – how does one give love when one has never received it oneself?

37

She, her sister and her niece are probably the highest-profile prisoners here – the wife and family members of a business tycoon accused of embezzling thousands of crores of small investors' monies. She is in her fifties, serene, efficient, instructing lawyers, writing down points from the chargesheet in the court lock-up. She wears a cotton salwar suit and sports a long ponytail. This elegant-looking woman, once an employee of her husband, is his second wife.

The niece is young, with an eight-year-old son, and more vulnerable and softer than her aunt. Her husband, like her uncle, is in the Main Jail. She describes how initially she did not want her son to be brought to jail for visits, feeling it would traumatize him. But now that it is close to ten months since her arrest and her bail has been rejected by the high court, his grandmother is bringing him to see her, and the child is being very mature about it. She says she was not very involved in business affairs and was much more into her family and social activities. From time to time officials from various enforcement agencies come to interrogate these prisoners in the small room next to the Mulakat Room.

These women, despite their wealthy background, seem to have adjusted remarkably well to imprisonment. Occupying one corner of Barrack No. 3, they manage to get most of their physical work done – buckets filled, clothes and bedding washed, and barrack duties carried out by distributing Canteen items to some of the needier prisoners. But they are also known to be helpful and generous, giving a sick prisoner some medicine, or biscuits to a child, or sharing food with someone who has been brought back late from the court or the lock-up. They also advise the less educated women about their legal remedies. One day in the lock-up, the niece exclaims frankly, 'I have learnt and understood so much about life after coming to jail, which I never could have otherwise.'

No doubt their path is smoothed by their capacity to pay. One cannot help but observe the small privileges they enjoy – like the amount of time they get to speak during the mulakat or the papers they are permitted to carry to court. (We UAPA prisoners are not even allowed to carry plain paper to take notes on.) But still I wonder, would their menfolk have mixed with ordinary prisoners so easily?

38

When this tall, big-built woman with her tiny bun says she has been convicted for twenty years for gangrape under the POCSO (Protection of Children from Sexual Offences) Act, we are shocked. Then she tells her story. It looks like she was involved in an extramarital relationship. Her husband's sister's minor daughter, who was living with them at the time, also began a relationship with a friend of her own lover. The scandal surfaced when the girl went home to her parents and her boyfriend tried to call her on her mother's phone number. Apparently, under family pressure, the girl testified that both the men – her boyfriend and her aunt's lover – had gangraped her and that 'her mami (aunt) had held her hands pinning her down and assisted them'.

This prisoner's husband is trying to divorce her now. Whereas, interestingly, it was she who had gone to court before all of this happened, accusing her husband and in-laws of domestic violence.

It's a sad story of an unhappy marriage, socially unacceptable love affairs and vicious legal revenge. Surprisingly, the two men accused in the case managed to get bail from the Supreme Court during the four years of the trial. But this woman, abandoned by her family, could not afford it. This is one of those cases in which even a feminist lawyer like myself is forced to look critically at rape laws that rely solely on the evidence of the prosecutrix.

39

This dark, plump woman with a chubby face, loud voice and rural accent is always cheerful, joking, singing songs and calling loudly across the ground to her friends in another barrack. Except when she is fighting – which she does with equal passion, loudness and stubbornness! One day someone asks about her husband. 'Oh, he? He must be having fun with his second wife,' she says. 'And children?' 'Oh, they are with my mother.' And the story comes tumbling out, helter-skelter.

Her husband had a mistress whom he almost beat to death and then drowned. His brother, being the sarpanch of the village, diverted the blame to her and her parents, and the two brothers gave evidence that she had had a fight with the mistress. Initially she was told, 'Don't worry, we'll get you out soon.' Her parents did get bail, but she ended up with a life sentence.

She says that when she was in Beed Jail and attending her trial at the Beed District Court, she would be taken to court with a group of gangsters from the men's section of the jail who often had their court dates on the same days as she had. Her 'bastard of a husband', as she put it, would allege that she was sleeping with those men in jail, unable to understand that this was not even possible. She remembers him saying, 'You were so thin, you have grown fat in jail, you are having fun with those men.' That was the last straw for her. She has given up on him. On the day of Vat Savitri Puja, when women go round a peepal tree seven times, praying for long lives for their husbands, she mocks them loudly, saying, 'I wish I could go around the tree in the opposite direction seven times and get rid of my husband!!' I recall seeing her doing a comic role in a skit for Women's Day, acting as a man and making us all laugh. There are many sorrows and hardships patiently borne behind that laughing exterior.

40

The big, frizzy-haired Nigerian woman in her T-shirt and close-fitting jeans has been released on bail just three or four days after entering jail. She and her boyfriend had been arrested for their involvement in fraudulent ATM withdrawals. But her presence has triggered off conversations about 'Negro prisoners' (blatantly discriminatory name-calling is, of course, common in jail, even if norms have changed outside its walls).

We are told there was a time, about a decade ago, when Barrack No. 4 of Yerawada Jail was exclusively occupied by prisoners of African origin. There used to be around twenty-five of them, most of them serving sentences under the harsh NDPS Act (Narcotic Drugs and Psychotropic Substances Act, 1985), which punishes possession of drugs, irrespective of intention, willingness or knowledge. Prisoners who have been here more than ten years recall that these African prisoners would have their food cooked separately and supervised by one of their own African Warders – mostly boiled meat and vegetables.

A Warder called Victoria, who had a daughter back home with whom she corresponded regularly, was not well. She had nearly completed her sentence and was looking forward to returning to her country. Tragically, she collapsed in the BC, and being a big-built woman, was half carried, half dragged to the Hospital Barrack. Soon the doctor arrived and declared her dead. Women say her body lay, covered in a sheet, near the Gate for several hours before it was taken outside the jail to the mortuary, and there was pin-drop silence in the jail. Everyone went into their barracks and no one had any food that night ... After this there were many enquiries, suspensions, officers coming in and out ... The practice of lodging African prisoners at Yerawada Jail for long periods of time was then discontinued.

41

You never see this thin, stern, poker-faced woman smile. She used to be a Warder of Barrack No. 4, where most occupants go to work in the fields and vegetable gardens of the jail in the daytime. Something about her behaviour had aroused suspicion, and what it was, was discovered in the jhadti of the barrack. She had accumulated a drum full of the most useless possessions – some twenty or twenty-five gunnysacks, many plastic mugs, dozens of jail soaps and shampoo pouches that were probably left over after distribution, many used utensils which those being released must have deposited to put back in the store, several pairs of chappals that had 'disappeared' earlier, and even bras and panties!

When she was shifted to Barrack No. 2, she virtually sat on dharna, and it took a good deal of scolding to actually move her. But nowadays we see her a little mellowed, and she is even babysitting an infant belonging to the barrack. It makes people remember the time four years ago when she was in charge of the BC and used to make tasty puranpolis (sweet rotis made on festive occasions in Maharashtra). She must have been a pleasanter person then.

I am left wondering about this peculiar jail version of kleptomania. Where does the urge come from to build up a treasure trove in jail, where there is no treasure and really no place to hide anything?

42

The elderly white-haired undertrial is sobbing inconsolably on the Stage while another woman, a cheery sort, tries to pacify her and wipes her tears as they wait for the Om Shanti sermon to begin. Her bail has been rejected by the sessions court.

She has been arrested for the suicide of her younger daughter-in-law. She is the mother of three sons. The eldest has a well-paying corporate job and spends a good deal of time with his wife and children in his own separate residence. The second had fallen on his head as a child and is intellectually disabled, and single. The third son is a policeman. She describes her daughter-in-law, the policeman's wife, quite objectively, as a good and intelligent girl but one who had many complaints about her husband, like his 'not giving time' and 'being aggressive and hot-tempered'. One day, this daughter-in-law strangled her baby son and then killed herself. She says her daughter-in-law's mother 'let the cat out of the bag' when she admitted to some neighbour that before killing herself, her daughter had phoned her in a panic saying she had killed the baby and 'now her husband would kill her'.

Her son, the policeman, has of course not been arrested. Someone has to go to jail, but it won't be him. He was away from home, and anyway the police are sympathetic to their own colleagues. The fact that his mother was in the house has been held against her, even though proximity by itself is not, legally speaking, critical. She cries, thinking of her disabled son, but doesn't see (or perhaps refuses to see) the role of her policeman son in the death of the young woman, or in her own incarceration.

43

We are travelling back from the court in the police van with this slim, well-educated, single woman in her early thirties. She is simply but elegantly dressed in a churidar-kurta and has her mehndi-dyed hair in a short ponytail. She has been in jail for eighteen months now. Her bail has been rejected thrice. The last time, it took eight months to be decided.

She was an employee in a cooperative banking and finance company and is charged with embezzlement and fraud while the eleven main accused – members of the board and senior managers – are all 'absconding'. She is sure that they are all in touch with the lawyer who appears for the company and for whom a lowly employee like her is obviously not a priority. She had been very upset earlier because these so-called 'absconders' had even been attending court on the appointed dates, after their applications for anticipatory bail were rejected by the high court, and yet they are not being arrested. Her colleagues, all retrenched now, come to meet her on court dates and are in complete solidarity with her. They had petitioned the authorities several times, demanding the arrest of the real culprits – the directors – who seem to have been adept at managing both the police and the prosecution. She describes how an outstanding loan she had taken, by pledging her personal gold ornaments, well before she worked for this company, is being used to deny her bail, even though it is unrelated to the company fraud.

Finally, today, the latest judge in a long series of judges hearing the case, has sacked the investigating officer, appointed a new one and directed that the absconding directors should be arrested and brought before the court in fourteen days. She is jubilant. 'Perhaps now I can get bail,' she says. 'How happy my mother will be.'

Postscript: When we meet her a month later, she says the senior managers/directors have got a stay from the high court on the order of the trial court. She is back to square one.

Routines, Rituals, Rains

The monsoon has arrived. We can hear the rain battering down on the tiles of the barracks all night, and it somehow makes our isolation a little more lonesome. But the trees are greening and the mosquitoes are back in earnest. The Constables now come for their Rounds in raincoats and gumboots, armed with umbrellas. Fortunately, the Phansi Yard is made of solid colonial stone, so it doesn't drip, but the damp patches in the plaster get larger and larger. The ground has become all squelchy and the children have to be content with racing down the covered corridors of the barracks and getting under everyone's feet. Prisoners don't have umbrellas, so they have to strategically rush to the Factory or BC or Canteen and the toilets/washrooms during the dry spells. The women who go to the Open Jail of course continue to work unfazed, stoically donning plastic sheets. The real challenge is drying clothes, particularly saris, and that is the bone of contention in most fights nowadays. In my cell I just spread out my clothes on the stone floor, request the Constable to put on my creaky fan and hope for the best.

Shoma Di and I always look forward to going to the Pune Sessions Court, even when it is raining, when it is messy and tiring to travel. The routine is all too familiar now: being strip-searched before leaving jail, waiting for a long time in the filthy court lock-up (our case is usually the last to be taken up), and wondering whether anyone has come to visit us and how impatiently they must be waiting . . . Finally, we are taken to the courtroom, flanked by our impressive array of women Guards (since we are UAPA detainees, a Constable invariably hauls a rifle and a Police Sub-Inspector carries a revolver in her holster). All of us co-accused look out for spouses, old parents and teenage children as we reach our court on the third floor, I for my daughter and my union comrades. Some Guards let us talk (or rather shout) to our visitors across a corridor; others insist it is against the rules. Sometimes we are allowed to accept food or tea from them, at other times sternly admonished if we do. My obviously working-class friends from the unions I work with, who have come all the way from Chhattisgarh, are treated more shabbily than the middle-class visitors. In fact, some are interrogated by the police afterwards. I rarely address the court, leaving that to my lawyers, but after learning of one such incident I was upset enough to stand up and complain to the judge. There are other challenges: while the rules allow us to talk to our lawyers, we always have to resist the efforts of the women Guards to either rush us back to jail as soon as the court has fixed the date for the next hearing, or back to the lock-up if our hearing is postponed until after lunch. In the meanwhile, we hear them on the phone constantly supervising their children remotely. Court duty is relatively easy duty, and if they can get through it quickly they can go home and rest. On many court dates, we spend the entire day in a room in the court, watching as the technicians of the Forensic Science Laboratory make 'clone copies' (at a snail's pace) of the large number of devices that have been seized from all of us. While we quite enjoy the break from the jail routine, our Guards are even more annoyed as they have to be with us the whole day. And, believe it or not, even five years down the line the process of copying and providing copies has not yet ended.

One day, as we sit in the police van waiting to be driven back to the jail, a Police Sub-Inspector (PSI) who is a stickler for the rules (perhaps extra careful because he is Muslim?) does not allow me to accept even a toffee (bought from the jail Canteen) from one of my co-accused. Much to his embarrassment, a very different scene is unfolding in the van parked alongside. Another prisoner, a 'gentleman don' dressed in a crisp shirt and jeans, with a tilak on his forehead, is sitting with his silk-sari-and-jewellery-bedecked family, all of them being feted with biryani packets, cold drinks and sweets by a bevy of hangers-on. Our PSI looks sheepish and says lamely, 'What to do, sometimes our own officers don't follow the rules . . .'

By now there are thirteen fat, spiral-bound volumes of the chargesheet and supplementary chargesheet in our case to keep me company in my cell. (A chargesheet details the accusations against the accused and contains the material relied upon by the prosecution to prove it.) The women Constables look at the tall pile (coming to just six inches below my shoulder) with disbelief. Wading through it and deciphering the Marathi officialese is a daunting task. While I have resigned myself to, and fallen into, the routine of jail life, that pile that I can always see from the corner of my eye tells me the depressing truth that we still can't see light at the end of the tunnel.

Shoma Di and I have subscribed to one newspaper each and exchange them in the evening before bandi. We read everything in the newspaper — it's our lifeline to the outside world. And, by the way, everything includes Calvin, the Sudoku and even the horoscope. The funny part is that anything to do with our own case is cut out of the papers. It is only from the big and small holes in them that we are able to make out that our case is making ripples and that people outside are making efforts for our release.

After many hearings in court I am allowed to receive five books a month during the mulakat. We aren't allowed to keep many books with us, so we exchange them amongst ourselves and then return them at mulakats. We devour them voraciously, a whole variety of authors – Baburao Bagul, Edward Snowden, William Dalrymple, Gautam Bhatia, Sharmila Rege, Yanis Varoufakis, Basharat Peer, Jerry Pinto, Amandeep Sandhu, Girish Karnad, A.G. Noorani, Prabhat Patnaik, Leo Tolstoy, B.R. Ambedkar, Rahi Masoom Raza, Charles Dickens. And we are delighted to receive an Agatha Christie omnibus. It has been a long time since I have read so much and so widely. It really helps to put one's ordeal into perspective. I am greatly impressed by the American feminist writer Naomi Klein's wonderful book, This Changes Everything: Capitalism vs Climate Change, *particularly her vivid descriptions of people's movements all over the world. I think of all the anti-displacement activists struggling in Chhattisgarh. They deserve to read this too, I feel, and begin translating it into Hindi, making copious explanatory notes. It gives me something meaningful to do.*

We try to settle into a routine, including exercising in our cells. What we especially look forward to is the precious half an hour outside the Yard, a time to walk, chat and even sing together – anything from women's liberation songs to songs from The Sound of Music … *(The two sisters don't like us singing inside the Yard, so I have given up even humming in my cell.)*

I spend a lot of time writing to my daughter, trying to respond regularly in a soothing manner to her sporadic letters full of distress, anger, resentment and loneliness. We are allowed letters only once in fifteen days, and both the incoming and the outgoing letters are vetted by the women Constables. It is largely a formality – the women don't know much English, for starters – but valuable time is lost, about a week each way. So by the time I respond, issues have already taken their toll and Maaysha has moved on. It is extremely frustrating.

Hailstorm

Today, after a really hot spell, there are showers. There's a cool breeze in the air laden with the aroma of wet soil, and the new tiles on the barrack roofs are shining brick-red. The trees look greener and the parched flower beds seem to be smiling. When the hailstones start banging on the tin roof of the Stage, the little children – all of their heads shaved recently by the jail barber – come out in the maidan to dance in this first rain and gather the little balls of ice. As the downpour thickens, the children are called back to the verandas of the barracks and everyone is watching the miraculous 'reincarnation' of nature. Some of the younger prisoners venture out to get soaked in the rain, collect hailstones and generally abandon themselves to this happy moment – this is the stuff happiness is made of in jail. If only society could 'reincarnate' itself like nature does, after a scorching summer of deprivation . . .

44

Over the last six or seven months, her little boy, born on Diwali day last year, has grown into a cute toddler with big kajal-lined eyes. Slowly, others have begun to handle him and look after him when his mother is busy with her chores. This young woman, barely twenty, came to Yerawada in an advanced stage of pregnancy. After her delivery we saw little of her, since she was allowed to wear a nightie and keep to the barrack nursing her baby. She usually wears a sari these days, and her hair is neatly plaited. I notice that she is always careful to keep herself and her child clean. The other day there was a mehndi competition and I saw her apply a beautiful design on another prisoner's palms and forearms.

I hear from her friend that she used to have a terrible temper, and one day hit her mother-in-law with a pressure cooker after being harassed by her. The old lady died, and she was arrested and jailed on her husband's complaint. His story is that she was involved with another man and his mother came to know. Paradoxically, he had also hired a lawyer for her, one whom she doesn't trust, and whom she has now swapped for a legal aid counsel. Recently she got a divorce notice from her husband, who apparently wants to remarry. By the way, this is a Muslim couple and he has not used either 'triple talaq' or 'bigamy' as a way out. Her friend advises her to strike a bargain: 'Tell him you will give consent if he takes back the case.' Meanwhile, she has other day-to-day problems. I hear her asking our yard-mate, 'Can't I get work in the agarbatti factory. I need a bit of Canteen stuff . . . my child asks others for biscuits and it's really embarrassing . . .'

45

Another prisoner, about ten years older than her, is also in jail for the murder of a family member. A classic Gujarati or Maharashtrian beauty, she's an expert dancer and carried with grace the costume she wore for the lavani (a seductive folk dance of Maharashtra) on 8 March – a large nathni, a gajra of flowers in her hair, a nine-yard silk sari. The other prisoners joke about the admiring looks she received from the male jail officers attending the programme. She is also the expert 'tailor' in the Factory. Many of the Constables are getting their salwar suits/blouses stitched by her to attend a colleague's marriage, for a fraction of the market rate. So she is in great demand with them.

But her own life has been tragic. She was married when she was just thirteen or fourteen, and now has a sixteen-year old daughter. After a loveless marriage of eighteen years with a jealous husband, she had an affair and ended up killing her husband in a confrontation. Her daughter is with her mother and brother while she serves her sentence.

When I first came to the jail, she and three other prisoners had been sent to Thane Jail for three months, to prepare for and participate in a dance programme organized by the jail authorities. It finally never materialized. Good performers at such programmes can earn a remission of one to three months in their sentence. That may not seem much in a conviction of fourteen years for murder ... yet the women toil hard even for this little concession.

So many of the cases of violence by women that I see here are evidently the outcome of years and sometimes decades of violence that they have suffered themselves. It reminds me of a film, *Provoked* (starring Aishwarya Rai and Nandita Das), in which a woman was finally acquitted of the murder of her husband in the UK because she was granted a plea of self-defence and grave provocation for the years of mental and physical torture she had been subjected to. But generally, in a criminal case in India, concession can only be given for a sudden provocation; anything else would be considered 'premeditated' and thus punishable.

46

She must be around fifty years of age, though quite sprightly, with a fair, freckled face. Her mehndi-coloured hair (mehndi, sold in the Canteen, is the standard hair dye here) is tied into a bun. She is one of those who willingly assists the Warder in the tougher physical tasks like washing the corridors, or smearing the mud platforms around the tree trunks with cow dung so that prisoners can use them as seats, or preparing the flower beds for fresh planting. She likes looking after the babies in the barrack too. But occasionally she gets into a shrill fight and we see abuses fly from both sides, like those strange astras in Ramanand Sagar's TV serial *Ramayana*. A murder undertrial, she has been here three years. One day, when she and other women are at work in the garden, some are called to the Dispensary, for routine HIV tests, it turns out. These tests, spoken of in hushed tones by prisoners, are usually seen as a 'morality check', and she is quick to piously say, 'Oh, I am not one of those . . .' Later I understand why she needed to say that.

A widow for a decade or more, she began a sexual relationship with a younger man, her neighbour, and her son – then in his early twenties – caught them together. The son was so enraged that he murdered the man, and both mother and son ended up in jail. Behind her back, other prisoners say, 'What was the need to jump into bed with someone?' 'And she – with a grown-up son – *chhi chhi*.' How unforgiving our society is of a woman's sexuality! In her place, a widower would have been persuaded to remarry because his sexuality is 'normal' and needs an outlet.

Today the woman has tears of joy in her eyes because her unforgiving son, who grudged her her relationship, has been released on bail. It was she who had arranged the cash for his bail from her bank account through her lawyer. Courts have enormous sympathy for men in such situations. I hope that in her statement to the police, in her eagerness to shield him, she hasn't taken most of the blame for a murder she didn't commit. What can otherwise explain his being released on bail, and her not? Is she punishing herself for her 'transgressions'?

47

Over the months, I have seen the periodic influx of batches of smart young girls, many from the North East and some even of foreign origin – Malaysian and Ukrainian. They are picked up during police raids at massage centres and spas, which Pune seems to have a lot of, and booked for soliciting. Some others, whom the police claim to have 'rescued', are sent to women's homes or to NGOs. The raids, I gather, are often reprisals by the police for not being paid hafta (regular bribe) or to make a show of moral outrage. I run into a single woman in her late twenties from the North East. Very quiet, soft-spoken and courteous. She usually wears a kurta and loose pyjamas with a stole. She had joined a massage centre as a receptionist three months earlier, and after a police raid the entire blame for managing the centre and its clients has fallen upon her. It seems a mobile registered in her name was being used to contact clients. Tellingly, her employer has not been arrested, but has engaged a fairly reputed lawyer for her. But naturally, the lawyer's primary interest is to save her employer, not her.

She has been in jail for about eight months now. Her father has come all the way from the North East to help her. He is neither rich nor well educated. He doesn't understand the local language and is staying in the city with great difficulty. I see him from the window of the Mulakat Room – a simple, anxious man, in his forties maybe. The sessions judge has dismissed her bail plea with simply one comment: 'She hails from the North East.' Is that a crime, or does he mean she cannot be trusted to produce a local surety? In the court lock-up with us, she sings a soulful Christian prayer in a very sweet voice, 'Thank you God, for looking after me.'

48

Every now and then I spot this wild young creature. She is dark and thin with big eyes and an untidy knot of curly hair, always dressed in garish churidar-kurtas and talking in a loud, aggressive voice. She seems to love to shock and scandalize people. When the Constable on guard in our Phansi Yard asks her, as she passes by, if she is married, she replies, 'Yes. I was married as soon as I got my MC. But my daughter is by another man. Is it necessary to stick with the same man all one's life?' She is a great one for getting into fights, and in the more than six months I have been here she has been shifted around to three different barracks. But she is actually a good worker and also likes looking after people, in a bossy sort of way. When five women enter the Hospital Barrack where she is lodged at present – all obviously rich rural folk arrested under the SC ST Atrocity Act (they get bail within a week, mind you!) – she takes them to the BC, to the bathhouse and around the jail to show them the ropes. 'Hey,' the Bai in our Yard shouts as she sees her aiming stones at the mango tree, 'stop that stone throwing immediately!' 'Just one more try,' she says cheekily and carries on. I am fascinated by this free spirit who won't allow herself to be bound down, rebellious but never bitter, in fact that rare rebel who can laugh and move on. When you meet people like that in jail you wonder what they might have achieved had things gone right for them.

49

Sometime ago, in the court lock-up, I met a young woman with a flashing smile who shook hands with everyone, saying: 'I will be released on bail by 14 April. That's our most important day you know – Baba Saheb's day.' (The fourteenth of April is the birth anniversary of Dr B.R. Ambedkar.) But she is still here. I spot her explaining at the Dispensary window that her middle name has been recorded wrongly, that 'X' is her ex-husband's name and 'Y' is her present husband's name. (In Maharashtra, not just the surname, but also the middle name of a woman is changed after marriage – earlier that would be her father's first name, and now it becomes her husband's first name. This creates immense confusion in today's digital age. I myself have had to insist at every place where names are recorded that I have just two names – Sudha and Bharadwaj – and nothing in between.)

This woman, her husband and her father have all been arrested for her ex-husband's death. The story I hear is that the man was an abusive drunkard and she had left him and gone to her parental home. Eventually, she got a divorce and remarried, and left her father's home to live with her present husband. Her ex, who would come drunk to her father's place and beg her to return, had come again as usual to her father's house – drunk and ill. Her father begged him to leave his daughter alone, told him she was happy and was living elsewhere. Later, when her father was going out, he saw the man lying semi-conscious on the road, a little way away from his house, and took him to hospital. She and her present husband also went there and tried to look after him. He died a couple of days later. And now all three of them have been accused of murder! Her lawyer says it's a straightforward case, that she should be out on bail soon . . . but it seems she is being punished for showing a little humanity.

Menstruation

In Odisha, when I had visited its prisons as a human rights lawyer several years ago, I remember recording many complaints of women about not being provided sanitary napkins. In Malkangiri, a town in Odisha, women were not only not provided napkins, but their toilets had no roof, and male sentries, pacing the high walls separating the Women's Jail from the men's section, could look right in.

So I was pleased to find that Yerawada had a much better system for menstrual hygiene. When women enter the jail, and regularly afterwards, their dates of menstruation are recorded. *(When one enters Byculla Jail one even undergoes a pregnancy test – so what if you are a senior citizen or have had a hysterectomy – rules are rules!)* Every month, menstruating women here are given cheap but hygienic cotton napkins. But when it comes to the disposal of napkins, things are not so enlightened. There is an incinerator that is never used because it can only be switched on once it's full; but it can't be full because no one is allowed to toss 'rotting and stinking napkins' into it in ones and twos! So effectively it is not used at all. Napkins are instead meant to be 'decently' disposed of in a pit on the jail boundary, to eventually be burnt. But remember, women are locked into their barracks from 5 p.m. to 7 a.m. It's a given that some napkins will be chucked carelessly at night. Every now and then someone's dirty napkin is found in the toilet or hidden in a corner, and pandemonium breaks out. Allegations and counter-allegations abound, and there are threats to strip all the inmates to check who is chumming (*once this was actually done in a Byculla barrack*). On one occasion, women were locked into a barrack for an extra half hour to extract a confession. ('Who left the napkin in a corner of the bathroom?') Watching from the sidelines, the solution seems simple: give women newspapers to wrap their napkins in and a separate garbage bin to chuck these into. But in jail, nothing is ever that simple. Rather than allowing prisoners to use the newspapers that are distributed two to a barrack, as well as those provided to prisoners like us, who pay for them from their PPC accounts, they insist that all newspapers have to be returned to the Gate at 7 a.m., to earn money from the waste collector, presumably! Another irrational, stupid and parsimonious rule. As Obelix would say, tapping his head: 'Piff piff! These Romans [read jail authorities] are crazy!!'

50

I miss seeing the pleasant, helpful woman from the BC who used to bring us our food. She has stopped coming to the Yard and has been sending someone else instead, because our yard-mates – the 'crazy sisters' – have taken a dislike to her friendly banter with us. A murder convict in her green-salwar kurta, this young Muslim woman in her late twenties is a regular worker in the BC. She's supposed to be an expert at making rotis. It is she who usually takes the sample thali of food from the BC to be tasted by Jailer Madam at her office. She has been convicted for killing her husband. Her brother has told her that he will not appeal and she must suffer her sentence. This is because he is married to her husband's sister, and that is the only way family peace can be maintained.

During the 8 March celebrations we saw another side of her – that she's a very good actor. Wearing a cap, tie, shirt and pants, and with her braid tucked away in a bun, she looked quite the handsome young man and kept the audience in splits with her comic turns. When I run into her today, she is excited – her brother had brought her children to see her after nearly eight years. 'Oh they are so grown up, my daughter so beautiful, my son so handsome . . .' She intrigues me, I wonder what made a person who seems so balanced commit such a crime. Abuse? An affair? Hers? His? What is her story?

Clothes

Convicts here get two green saris, two white blouses and two white petticoats. This eliminates the need for underclothes for those who can't afford to have them sent from home. I do see some women wearing green salwar-kurta and green dupattas. But I am told that they date back to a period when stitching was being taught at the Factory and the trainees stitched sets for themselves and their friends. Right now, the only option for a convict is to wear a sari. All the clothes are of cotton, a sensible choice, except in the rainy season when clothes don't dry easily and there is not enough space to dry them.

Every fifteen days or so, the godaam in the Hospital Barrack is opened and those women whose clothes have got worn out/torn can line up to get new saris/blouses/petticoats, but only in exchange for their old ones. These are likely to be recirculated after washing, perhaps given to the most indigent prisoners, and if worn out or torn beyond repair, they are eventually burnt. Of course, the give and take is not all fair. Some women may manage to smuggle out more than two sets or get better or fresher clothes.

One day, just as the monsoon is beginning, we see the women being lined up outside Barracks 1 and 2, each wearing one set of clothes and holding another in their hands. Jhadti is going on, and all extra sets are being made into huge bundles and being carried away to the godaam. What perfect timing! Just when everyone desperately needs extra clothes in the rainy season . . . but that's what jail is like – irrational.

Undertrials accused under Section 302 (murder) have to be dressed in green prison clothes, as I have mentioned earlier. It seems to be a practice peculiar to Maharashtra. It is probably to 'single them out' for their 'potential to be dangerous'? Even when they go to Sassoon Hospital they wear green, and are thus distinguishable from other patients. But obviously, the practice has no legal sanction because when they go to court they are allowed to wear their 'civil clothes'. At least in court they are still considered innocent till proven guilty.

51

I have noticed that the group most openly referred to in a derogatory manner here are the Pardhis. They are a branch of the same denotified nomadic tribe that is also found in Madhya Pradesh and Chhattisgarh. They have a complicated history: in British times they were so rebellious and difficult to suppress that they were notified as 'criminal tribes'. After Independence this discriminatory tag was supposedly removed by 'denotifying' them. But in effect, not much has changed. In the very same session of Parliament in 1952 that the Criminal Tribes Act was repealed, a Habitual Offenders Act was enacted to perpetuate precisely the same prejudice.

In the police lexicon, members of such tribes are 'natural suspects' and therefore routinely rounded up for any petty crimes, particularly thefts in their jurisdiction. It is the simplest way to 'solve' a crime. The Pardhi men, women and children are known for their dancing, singing and acrobatic performances. It's quite possible that some are involved in petty theft, but often not in the other serious offences of which they are routinely accused. The more serious problem is that because of the prejudice against them, they can rarely get other sorts of employment.

The group here consists of a round, fat Pardhi woman with two younger, skinny women in tow. They come in shabby but not unclean clothes, and are quite vocal about their turns at the drinking water taps and the line for bhatta. They stick together. And that is probably quite necessary, otherwise they would never get their chance. They have come in with two children. One, an emaciated and obviously malnourished child who can sit but cannot crawl or walk, despite being one and a half years old, and another a five-day-old child looking small and red. The baby has fever and a rash. One day, Shoma Di and I are happy to see them standing at the Gate. They have got bail, it appears, from the way their names are called. But they are back the next day, having been slapped with MCOCA. What sort of 'organized crime' could these obviously impoverished women have been engaged in?

Now the elder child has been given to a relative outside. The little baby has picked up fairly well, and like all babies has become a cute plaything. One day, while returning from filling up our drinking water, we find the mother wailing loudly. What's happened, everyone asks her in alarm? 'Someone has stolen my chappals,' she cries. These are the same rubber chappals that cost just Rs 125 in the Canteen. So much for being a 'member of an organized crime syndicate'.

52

Another woman, with a beautiful round face like a full moon, hailing from a Hindi-speaking denotified tribe, has become a Christian in jail. I hear her story from another prisoner, narrated in an unsympathetic and contemptuous tone. It seems the woman and her husband had borrowed Rs 30,000 from a contractor. When they couldn't repay the loan, he started demanding that she sleep with him. After complying in terror for a few days, the husband and wife killed him. Clearly, they were not very 'seasoned' criminals, for they left the corpse in their own jhopdi (hut), locked the hut and fled with their baby daughter ... Naturally, they were caught. The daughter is about five years old now. When I ask the child at the water tap, 'What happened at court today?', she replies smartly, 'Nothing ever happens. Only dates ... *Tareeq pe tareeq.*'

Her mother, wearing the green sari of a murder undertrial, works so hard that it almost seems like penitence. She makes rotis in the BC, a tedious job involving being close to the fire for long periods. She is always stern with her daughter, who, after being harshly scolded and beaten, sometimes goes off to be cuddled by the elderly deaf convict who works as a bageechewali or gardener. The child is very smart, independent, and a leader of the kids in mischief-making, but her mother seems worn out with worry. Once in the Thursday Bible session, I see her, with closed eyes, clutching her Bible close to her, praying fervently ... The film character PK would have exclaimed: 'What's the use when it's a wrong number?'

53

When I first spotted her from afar – a Warder in Barrack No. 2 – this big-built Bengali woman, with her topknot covered by her yellow Warder's sari, I saw her only as a bully. And we all know how and why bullies are always made class monitors. She was shouting in a Bengali–Marathi–Hindi khichdi lingo, which I later became quite enamoured of: '*Chala, bandi la, imaandaari se chala . . .*' (Hurry up, it's bandi time, now go in without a fuss) while herding along her reluctant wards. I have also seen her slap a really sad-looking but argumentative prisoner pretty hard. (The fact that that was taken very casually by all concerned was frightening.) But over time we have come to see other sides of her. Despite being stout, she's an excellent and swift-footed dancer, and performed beautifully in the 8 March dances.

I hear her story in bits and pieces. She is from a Hindu upper-caste family, and eloped with a Muslim man. Her relations with her family have been severed. 'After all, I disgraced my mother, cut off her nose,' she says laughingly. She came here some sixteen years ago. Her daughter was born in Byculla Jail and is in a sanstha now.

Currently she is the Warder of the BC. When the Ramzan fast is being observed, it is a gruelling task for her, involving getting up at 2 a.m. and distributing the sehri (dawn meal) at 3.30 a.m., in addition to the regular duties of overseeing the doling out of breakfast, bhatta, bananas, etc., and bringing food to us in the Phansi Yard, which she does herself. Since Shoma Di is Bengali and I too understand the language, an intimacy has developed between us, and she sometimes unburdens herself to us. We notice that she is very good with infants, and some of the Constables happily use her as a 'one-woman creche' when they bring their kids to the jail. She feeds and bathes a favourite ward, carries her around and amuses her ... all presumably done for free and taken for granted too.

Nowadays she looks forward to being sent to the Open Jail; that means being sent to the jail fields to work. This will earn her a remission of sentence. She may even be released in a year. Her partner had gone to the Open Jail some years back and has been released. He keeps promising to come for mulakat but hasn't turned up yet. Men! They are both accused of murdering her bhabhi. But she is quick to say, 'Actually he is innocent, he only suffered the sentence for my sake.' Women!

Roza

The rozas (fasts) began in the extremely hot days of May and are now at their tail end. Given how hard at work communal forces are beyond the gates of Yerawada Jail, it never ceases to surprise me how naturally the jail adjusts to the month of Ramzan. At the moment fifty-odd of the 280 prisoners are fasting, and mind you, many of them are not Muslim (though it is true that a disproportionate number of convicts are Muslim). Not drinking water until iftaar at 7 p.m. must be sheer torture. The opening of the BC at 2 a.m. by the night-shift Constables and the delivery of sehri by the Mess workers from barrack to barrack happen like clockwork. It is the usual rice and chapatti, but since the sabzi is made for fewer people and has to be made dry to last, it's usually more tasty than usual. And they also get tea to wash it down with. Those who are observing the fast collect their quota of milk at 7 a.m. and their evening bhatta at 4.15 p.m. with everyone else, but they wait till after the bandi and a special 7 p.m. sounding of the Toll for the iftar. In the barracks, groups of rozedaars gather together and make special dishes. Fruit salad and milk/ curd is a favourite, since fruits are sold thrice in the month to those who can afford them. Another is 'fried rice', made with rice, pickle oil, farsan (Gujarati snacks) and chopped onions and tomatoes; and rolls made of chapattis filled with crushed peanut paste and the green chilli thecha (chutney) sold in the Canteen, or sweet rolls made of chapattis and jam.

All the non-vegetarian prisoners look forward eagerly to the chicken at Eid, prepared by the Muslim prisoners in the Main Jail. Having been told it is delicious, Shoma Di and I quickly sign up for it, and the cost is deducted from our PPC account. And there is sheer qurma too, for everyone, a bit watery, but with a bit of luck one can get some raisins and pieces of kaju (cashew nuts).

It feels strange that religious rights are conceded so freely in jail but other kinds of collective activity are looked upon with great suspicion and in fact flatly discouraged. The jail authorities nurse a morbid fear of any kind of organizing or unionizing. Perhaps this is in continuity with the colonial times, when the rulers did not interfere with 'native customs' but stamped down hard on political rights.

And indeed, Yerawada is a very old jail built in 1871, and

the Main Jail has wards named after Gandhi, Tilak, Nehru, etc., who were imprisoned here many times during the freedom struggle. In fact, many important political meetings took place here, which the British allowed, despite their aversion to political rights. One of them preceded the historic Poona Pact, which in my opinion was unfair to the absolutely valid concerns of Dr B.R. Ambedkar and was brought about by a sort of emotional blackmail by Gandhiji. Such meetings being facilitated (say for jailed Opposition leaders to meet and discuss things) would be unthinkable for today's independent Indian government.

54

When we saw her from a distance through the bars of Phansi Yard, she looked like a very thin version of Indira Gandhi, with her beaked nose and streak of grey hair, though in her case it was tied up in a ponytail. We noticed that this very middle-class looking person did a lot of physical work – carrying buckets of water, transporting tins of gravel on her head to repair the pathways, helping old women shift their belongings from one barrack to another. It turned out that this universal man Friday was an 'old hand' in this prison and had been implicated in some fifteen or sixteen cases of petty theft over the past fourteen years. When she was sentenced for the first time in 2004 or 2005, she insisted that the Guards take her back to court to demand that her four-year-old daughter be given an education under State supervision and at State cost till she became a major. We discover that that child is now nearly eighteen years old, stays in a boarding school, and that she is very proud of her. 'So much cleverer than me and more beautiful too,' she says. 'Why should she ruin her life with me?'

She's served her sentence in one case and has been acquitted in the rest. Ironically, the case in which she is currently arrested is false. She was working at the house of a nagarsevak (a municipal councillor) and was accused of stealing a gold chain. Later, as is quite clear from the record, the chain was recovered from that very house. Yet she has been in jail for eight months and wasn't taken to court for five successive hearings. On our way back from our last court date, she travelled with us in the same police van and said she was thinking of pleading guilty. She had already done six months plus another two months in lieu of a fine, and the judge had said he would set her free. 'Why don't you try to get bail?' I asked, a little naïvely. She said, 'I have already told the jail's legal aid lawyer, she had said she would file my application for bail, but nothing has happened so far.' The police guard with us had a different take. She said, 'Hey, don't plead guilty. The moment you come out, they'll slap a few more theft cases on you. You're better off in jail.' Suddenly, the prisoner asks me, 'Aunty, can you please give me your black churidar. I only have one salwar and it's torn. I don't get any money order or anything. My mother is no more and I am a widow. I just get Canteen stuff by doing someone's chores for them.' Grudgingly, I admire her spunk. Nothing seems to faze her, despite the fact that the choice she faces is between the devil and the deep blue sea.

55

We already know her news before she is brought back into the lock-up from the court. The Guard has told us she's been sentenced for life. We are all a little anxious – will she break down? But though she is tense, she is still in denial mode. 'How can it be? There was no argument by prosecution or defence. There is no evidence. I will get released in a few months by the high court.'

This tall woman, with a long, jet-black ponytail, is not your usual prisoner. She is a police Constable who has been convicted for the murder of her pregnant mami (her maternal uncle's wife). The rumour machine has it that she was romantically involved with her mama, though she was herself married, with a child. She is supposed to have stabbed the mami to death. But according to her, there is no evidence.

At Yerawada for the past two–three years, she has been drawing the half pay of a suspended employee. Her barrack-mates dislike her for her arrogance. She refuses to do any barrack duties and also cocks a snook at the jail authorities. She has been preparing for the civil services examination and manages to get more books to keep in her barrack than other book lovers like us. An inveterate cribber, she has repeatedly approached the court with complaints against the jail. Confident that she will be acquitted, she has told us that once she is released she will continue to pursue her complaints against the Investigating Officer and Superintendent of Police. Among other things, she has accused them of looting money and valuables from her – which might well be true. Her father is an army man; perhaps that explains why he supports her stubborn litigation and sense of entitlement.

Now that she is no longer an undertrial but a convict, she has to stand afresh at the Gate during the Saturday Round when the Superintendent and other officers come for their inspection. There she stands, displaying her Convict Card, in the line at the Gate along with the new admissions. She had thought her jail journey would end soon, but a new and perhaps more difficult phase has started.

Corporal punishment

I often hear that prisoners used to be regularly beaten earlier in this jail, and that 'habitual offenders' were beaten on admission itself to 'break them in', as one 'breaks in' animals. That is not the norm at Yerawada today. The younger Constables have not seen such conduct and have been trained in a different culture. They would rather scold, show sternness and threaten to complain to their superiors or to the court to enforce discipline. Some of the older ones, though, speak nostalgically about the 'harder discipline' of the old days. They are also looser-tongued in their anger, particularly in the use of explicit abuses.

In the several months I have been here, I have come across only one case of a Constable seriously beating someone. As usual, there was a fight over scarce water. A prisoner was washing her clothes in a bucket near the water tank and some of the soapy water fell into another woman's clean water bucket. This second woman, elderly and known to be cantankerous, responded with a steady torrent of abuse. One of the young Constables first tried to outshout her. When the elderly lady didn't stop, she slapped her hard and pushed her down. When the woman began to protest, she kicked her with her booted foot. Meanwhile, the daughter of this old woman – also a convicted prisoner and quite sharp-tongued herself – got to know. She had just come in from the Open Jail where she had been working. She accosted the Constable and shouted at her. Other Constables gathered around and held the prisoner back by her arms, but not before she too was slapped. The jail was abuzz with tension, with women muttering among themselves that 'the old woman has no control over her tongue and that particular Constable is known to be hot-headed'.

Before the bandi, all the prisoners of Barracks 1 and 2 were asked to bring one bucket each into the barrack, and all extra buckets were to be deposited in the godaam to avoid water fights. (What an irrational solution in the face of a serious water crisis!) Later I heard that a delegation of older prisoners went to the Jailer to explain that the fight had nothing to do with the filling of buckets and that this step would only make things worse. The Constable has never been publicly chastised, but hopefully she was reprimanded in private.

Later, at Byculla Jail, I gathered that a lot of the chastening of the behaviour of the women Constables there and in other women's jails in Maharashtra has happened because of the notorious case of the death of Warder Manjula Shetty in June 2017 in Byculla Jail.

Shetty was beaten to death by the jail staff. After her death, there was what media called a 'prison riot'. What actually happened was that the prisoners boycotted all meals and protested vehemently till an FIR was registered against the Jailer and five women Constables at 10.30 p.m. the next day. Last I heard, these six were facing a murder trial and had not yet been released on bail.

While I was in Byculla, the chargesheets of the counter case of 'rioting in the jail' that had been filed against thirty-odd prisoners who protested Manjula's death were being handed to the seven accused still present there in 2021, and I got a chance to see all the records.

The description of the killing by the complainant and witnesses in the chargesheet is horrifying. Manjula, then aged about thirty-eight, had come from Yerawada Jail three months earlier. She had completed thirteen years of a fourteen-year sentence and had just a few months to go.

According to the witnesses, on that fateful day Manjula had been distributing eggs and pav, and two eggs and five pavs were found to be missing. The Jailer had shouted at her, and perhaps Manjula had been rude and impertinent too. Later, the six jail staff had stripped her, kicked and punched her, and beaten her with lathis in the small office at the entrance to the women's jail compound. Her screams were heard by other prisoners as they lined up in the compound to collect their bhatta. Then the jail staff wrapped Manjula's green sari round her neck and dragged her to her barrack, Barrack No. 5 on the first floor, where they beat her again. Manjula was bleeding and lay semi-conscious in the barrack. At 7 p.m. she asked to be taken to the toilet. While excreting, urinating and bleeding all at once, she fainted. The women shouted and shouted for the Jail Doctor to be called. She was taken to the JJ Hospital, where she was declared brought dead.

Whether the complainant and witnesses in Manjula's case will decide to compromise because of the counter case of rioting and the accused jail staff therefore let off lightly, one doesn't know. But the brave insistence by the prisoners after Manjula's death on registering an FIR has certainly had its impact.

56

She's a thin elderly Muslim woman, clearly from a labour family. Like other rural Muslims, she wears a sari, a faded synthetic one, when she goes to court. She was arrested just before Ramzan and is observing roza in jail. We are waiting in the court lock-up to be taken to court. Her middle son was married just a month ago. She says they are a poor family and everyone has to work hard to make ends meet. The middle son is a daily-wage labourer, like his elder brother and father, and they don't have land of their own. She feels that her new daughter-in-law, for whose death she is in jail, was probably not ready for the marriage or had been in love with someone else. She says she had simply told her not to go too far away to wash clothes and had given her some work to do in the house. That day, only the two of them were in the house. Later, she says, she found that the daughter-in-law had hanged herself. She, her husband, and both her elder sons have been arrested. The youngest one, a schoolgoing lad, is alone at home for Eid. She weeps for him. After court she tells us, 'My husband and eldest son have got bail. Inshallah, I will get it too. But we have to arrange sureties . . . We are so poor.' I still see her in jail months later.

The process of being actually released even after a bail order is passed is really tedious in Maharashtra. I remember how many times in Byculla Jail I would prepare lists of all those who had got bail but were unable to either pay cash or furnish sureties. If a person is standing surety for an amount of more than Rs 15,000, that person has to get a solvency certificate from the concerned tehsildar. And usually, what is demanded is 'a local surety' (someone with property in the same district). What do persons who hail from other states – like myself – do?

57

I am surprised to see a doctor here who has been sentenced for ten years for causing death by negligence. Negligence is a difficult thing to prove legally, and middle-class people usually have enough access to good lawyers to get the benefit of the doubt.

Besides, the judiciary tends to be more sympathetic to those they recognize as being from their own class. I remember once arguing for cancelling the bail of a surgeon who I believe to be squarely responsible for the death of twelve young women in a government hysterectomy camp. He had carried out eighty-three operations in three and a half hours with a single laparoscope, not giving enough time even for sterilization of the instrument between surgeries. All the women, mostly from poor village families and mothers of little infants, had died of septicaemia. But the branch of the Medical Council of India in our state – Chhattisgarh – had threatened to go on strike in support of the surgeon, who had got an award the previous year for doing a record number of hysterectomies. He was released on bail and finally discharged because he successfully argued that, though a retired person, he had worked in a government capacity and no sanction had been granted by the government for his prosecution.

But to come back to the prisoner, she is a tall and slightly stooped lady in her fifties, with shoulder-length greying hair. Apparently, she was here as an undertrial and was let out on bail, but is back now as a convict. She may, on appeal to the high court, get a suspension of her sentence. I hear her telling her story – or at least her side of the story – to one of the Constables. (The Constable knows her because she had taken her own sister to this doctor once.) A patient was bleeding heavily, she says, and despite advice to her family to organize blood for her transfusion, they had failed to do so. In fact, they abandoned the patient for some time. I know how fearful people still are of donating blood, so this may well be true, though probably not the whole story. After the patient died, not only this doctor and her husband, who ran the nursing home, but even the non-medical staff had been arrested. The latter were released on bail later, and I presume subsequently acquitted. What I notice is that she seems to have taken her conviction with grace. She doesn't have a fixed 'group' but joins some of the older convicts for her meals. The other day I was quite happy to see her advising a young convict about some medical problems. And she has been called to the Dispensary to help in routine blood pressure examination for the chronic hypertensives among us. At least her skill and knowledge are being put to some use.

58

Today was a day of bad news. In the morning, a young woman in Barrack No. 2 was told during mulakat that her father had passed away. She was half dragged, half carried by others to the veranda of the barrack, where she began lamenting loudly. 'He came only fifteen days back, and he wasn't even ill, how can this be? Oh God, why have you done this to me?' She was beating her breast in mourning. Other women gathered around her. One held her to her bosom, while others tried to speak words of reassurance. Someone brought water, another began weeping herself in sympathy, perhaps recollecting some private grief of her own. There is mourning in Barrack No. 1 too; someone has been told that her mother died. When something like this happens, we are all filled with dread and anxiety about our respective loved ones whom we can only communicate with sporadically.

But the worst news comes to us in the court lock-up. Our smart young lady Constable on duty outside the lock-up gets a phone call from the ICU of Sassoon Hospital: 'Hey, that little boy's aaji (grandmother) has died.' We are all shocked. This aaji has been at Yerawada for the past four–five months with her grandson, who is about seven years old. She, her husband and her son have been convicted for the burning to death of her daughter-in-law. They were here earlier too, as undertrials, when the child was a baby, but had been released on bail. Now, six or seven years later, they are back here as convicts. I wonder if the child ever realized the irony of his situation, of being looked after by a grandmother accused of killing his mother. It seems that the daughter-in-law's family, who lodged the complaint, didn't ask for custody of the child. His grandmother has burn marks on her chest and her son has a burnt arm. (This could be because they burnt the daughter-in-law, or because they were, as they claim, rescuing her.) The old woman was found to have several blockages in her heart and was to be operated on shortly. We had even heard that she had got bail on medical grounds, but it could not be executed because it wasn't clear who would care for her and for her grandson if she went out. And now she is dead.

The next day I see the boy playing with all the other kids, oblivious of the storms buffeting his future. Since a man can't keep a child (even a male one) with him in jail, the boy will have to be sent to a sanstha perhaps, or be handed over to a relative through the court. (How patriarchal a system this is, that does not credit a father with any capacity for parenting!) It is Eid today, and the Muslim Warder who has been looking after the boy ever since his grandmother was admitted to the hospital has bathed him and applied kajal to his eyes. She holds him close to her when he sleeps at night. Sometime around noon, the call comes to send him for his grandmother's last rites; his father is waiting outside with the police escort. A bunch of women go to kiss and hug him, and bid him goodbye.

Many more are watching, like we watch him from the bars of our cage. As he goes to the Gate with his little cloth bag of belongings, the Warder and so many others are in tears.

59

She's a lady in her late fifties, stodgy and short with snub features and greying hair. Not stone deaf, for she is quick to hear criticism, but pretty deaf nevertheless. She's been here for four or five years now after her conviction and works as a bageechewali. That means she can stay out in the afternoon bandi, carrying tins of water to water the plants in the hot summer days and zealously guarding the mangoes in the 'mango days'. She claims to only gather fallen mangoes for the BC people to make mango panna (juice) and pickle (the first for the Madams and the second for the BC staff). But she also gets her favourite stone-throwers to aim at mangoes for herself. Meanwhile, you can hear her screechy voice yelling at all the other stick- and stone-throwers. She is the natural harbour of the little ones – aaji par excellence – and even rescues the not-so-little ones when they are being thrashed or scolded by their mothers.

The bageechewali says her husband was a Class IV employee, and after his retirement he would take on rent plots of land and cultivate grapes and other fruits. 'I never had to work in those days,' she says. 'He's no more now.' Her daughter-in-law burnt to death. Though I can well imagine her as a screechy, harassing mother-in-law, it is also true that she and her son were not present at the time of the incident. Her son, probably as much a harasser as she, came home drunk later. When he was detained by the police, he blamed his mother, maybe to save himself, though the daughter-in-law did not even mention her in her dying declaration. At the end of it all, the old woman is in jail and the son has been acquitted. 'I just do this gardening work to get by,' she shrugs. This is, of course, in reply to a completely different question which I ask and she hasn't heard.

60

This plump but tall and beautiful young Muslim woman with rosy cheeks and tweezed eyebrows and a lovely Urdu lahja (style), is childishly confiding, telling us everything about herself on our very first trip to court together. Her husband was one of a group of nine who participated in some bank fraud, and he is absconding now. She says she missed him so much that she joined him for some time when he was a fugitive. But then she got the shocking news that her mother had passed away. Her husband tried very hard to dissuade her from attending the funeral, but she insisted on going. The police arrived in burqas at her house the very next morning and arrested her. Though they interrogated her for a long time, she says she could not give them much information since she knew nothing about the fraud. But since the WiFi subscription that was used to carry out fraudulent online transactions is in her name, and so are the properties her husband purchased with the moolah, she's what you might call an 'innocent accomplice'. Many women are held here almost as judicial hostages for their criminal husbands, fathers and boyfriends. But she remains in love with her husband. 'He is feeling very bad that I'm in jail. He'll try to get me out somehow,' she says. I hope so too.

The Bais

How can any description of jail be complete without talking about the Bais or the women Constables? There are all types here – the quiet and the talkative, the ambitious and the laid-back, the friendly and the arrogant. The ones in their twenties are mostly from rural backgrounds, and many of them are appearing for their graduation or postgraduation examinations in the hope of promotions. They are usually not English-speaking. Ironically, their backgrounds are quite close to those of many of the prisoners here. Had it not been for the uniform that stands between them, many friendships could have been struck up.

Most of the younger women are negotiating complicated situations in their own lives – getting married, having babies, adjusting with in-laws . . . In my time here, I have seen four Bais go off on leave to get married. At such times, the conversations between them as they pass each other on Duty Rounds are centred on saris and blouses, menus for wedding dinners, and what gifts to give their colleagues. In the marriage season, almost every Bai has a sari blouse being stitched at the

Factory for a small fee. A young woman convict who is an expert tailor is perhaps the most sought-after person in the jail to discuss designs with and to be inundated with requests to 'Pleeeeease finish mine first!' The night-duty Bais have no problem getting their hands decorated with mehndi – all it takes is to have a talented prisoner sit near the gate of the barrack and for the Bai to pass her hands and the mehndi cone through the bars!

The working conditions of these women are easy in some respects and pretty tough in others. Their shifts are twelve-hour long, either day or night, with one short break at night, and a longer one during the day. They have a day off every week, which is not necessarily a Sunday, when their families usually have the day off. So they often do continuous duty to accumulate days of leave and be with their families. They are also transferred to other jails in Maharashtra every three years. This means that a lot of them live in quarters near the jail, alone or in pairs, and only go home to their villages once in fifteen days, maybe combining two weekly offs. It also means that once their babies are off breastfeeding, they are often handed over to maternal/paternal grandmothers. Sometimes husbands who are in private service will adjust their holidays to come and live with their wives. All this means considerable reorganization of family duties and expectations. Obviously, a government job is worth this adjustment, even for the most patriarchal of families, but most Bais still have to do a lot of juggling between home and work, and bear a heavy double burden.

In all the time I've been here, I have met only one Bai who didn't have marriage as her aim, who valued her independence and said she was in no hurry to get 'tied down'. And yes, one who has actually had a secret inter-caste marriage, with the help of her friends among the jail staff, but has only declared it recently and is waiting for the families to accept it.

When these Constables get noticeably pregnant, they swap their smart khaki shirt-pants, cap and boots for a khaki-coloured sari and sandals and usually work till their eighth month. Most avail of their six-month pregnancy/maternity leave after that. They are allowed to continue wearing saris till their babies are a year old, presumably to facilitate breastfeeding. They are also exempt from night duties till the baby is one year old.

The Constables undergo fairly rigorous training in one or the other jail campus at the start, incorporating exercise, theory classes and self-defence. They are also rotated between the Main Jail (for males) and the Women's Jail. In the Main Jail they may be allotted to the mulakat section, the computer section, the Canteen, the BC, the Showroom or the towers from where they keep a watch on different sections of the jail from above. In the Women's Jail they are appointed at different spots in the Undertrial and Convict Compounds, at the BC, the Factory, the Gate, the Dispensary, the Open Jail, the Canteen, the Mulakat Room, and the Office, in rotation.

This being a women's jail, one great convenience is that some Bais with breastfeeding infants bring them to work and have them looked after by some of the older, more responsible prisoners. I doubt that this is a 'legal' arrangement, but it happens frequently. Even older children sometimes come in with their mothers (and grandmothers!) among the staff on

Sundays or in the evenings to play on the swings and merry-go-round. Actually, this situation should be legalized by there being a proper creche in the jail and actual appointment of some prisoners to babysit.

What is very disappointing is that most of the Bais and other jail staff don't have any idea of the reformative role that modern prisons are supposed to play. They do the discipline part well enough – the locking in, the counting, the searches. But in the handling of disputes, their approaches are usually along the 'natural' fault lines of power. They calm the women down in a superficial way, never getting to the root of the matter. They also behave in an untrained way with prisoners with psychological problems – sometimes mocking them or dealing harshly or contemptuously with them and in fact compounding the problem. Whether or not counselling is part of their training, it definitely doesn't make its presence felt in practice.

Jhadti

The biggest shock on entering jail is being subjected to a strip search. A thorough search not only means taking off all one's clothes, including underclothes, but also doing squats to show that nothing has been inserted into one's private parts . . . Also one is expected to open one's braid or hair bun to show that nothing has been hidden in the hair. All ornaments, wristwatches, etc., are of course confiscated and kept away at the stage of admission itself. These searches also happen each time we leave for and return from court. Over several months, the shock recedes. One even becomes quite nonchalant about stripping in front of the other three or four prisoners who are being taken to the court in the same van. The thoroughness of the search depends on the mentality and mood of the senior Constable on duty. Many don't like seeing prisoners completely naked and ask them to replace their upper clothing before they take off their lower clothing.

There are other kinds of searches too. Jhadti, a word that encompasses every kind of search, is a regular and humiliating feature of jail life. Barracks are searched at least weekly, if not more frequently. And sometimes there are surprise searches. All prisoners are called out at closing time and the Constables file into the barrack, with their boots on. They open out all the rolled beddings, tip out the contents of all the bags, helter-skelter, on to the floor. Usually they wear hankies over their mouths and leave with expressions of distaste writ large on their faces, shampooing their hands to wash themselves clean.

What do they look for? Pieces of rope or twine, anything sharp that can be used as a weapon – scissors, knife, spoon, blade, sharpener, nail cutter – rotting food that people have stashed away, extra sets of clothes – you are only allowed two sets and at most a third 'good' one for court . . . Often they encounter dirty bedding or clothes that haven't been washed. All such items, never mind if anyone protests, are carried out in a sack. Then the women file past for a body check and pat-down before they return to sort out the terrible mess and fight vociferously over missing toothpaste tubes or bottles of pickle.

For us in the high-security Phansi Yard, the jhadti is a twice-daily routine, at opening and closing. Theoretically, that means the entire cell is searched twice a day. In practice, however, it becomes more of a ritual – we show them our tidily folded bedding, get a quick pat-down like the sign of the cross made over our bodies, and a hand passed over the bars at the back of the cell. Just a check that we are well and truly locked in. But sometimes the search is conducted under the eagle eye of the Jailer Madam . . . 'Why so many books?' 'Do you really need this enormous chargesheet?' 'Put away the extra set of clothes . . .' 'Dahi is not allowed, no fermented foods.' 'But Madam,' I reply, 'the packet of milk gets spoilt, so . . .'

Winter Again

The Darkness Within

On 1 November, I mark my second birthday in custody. Diwali was in late October this year, and Shoma Di has saved a bit of her Diwali faral (snacks, in Marathi) as a treat for me. She gives me a beautiful card with a hand-drawn Sudoku on the front and a ballerina 'dancing away to her freedom' on the inside. It's an ode to my Sudoku mania.

When I was 'outside', I would do Sudokus on the long metro rides from my home in Faridabad to the National Law University in Dwarka, where I was teaching, or to escape from the depressing news in the newspaper, but only the easy ones. It seemed such a waste of time to bother with the tough ones. In jail, time passes at a tortoise's pace and I have become an expert at the tough Sudokus. I do it the long-hand way, filling pages with the 9x9 grids and working out the alternatives. Now I can do nearly all the Sudokus in both our newspapers – including the 'Hard' and 'Extreme' ones. Numbers are reassuring things – they are neither left wing nor right wing, they don't change with governments, with freedom or bondage. You only need to focus on the digits 1 to 9 being in the right place.

So much has been happening in this one year, of which we can only hear echoes, see shadows. The Modi government has been re-elected at the Centre, and a new Congress government has come to power in Chhattisgarh. Article 370 has been abrogated, a new Citizenship Amendment Act has been passed that is seeing widespread protests . . . It feels so strange to be out of touch with political developments. I miss my trade union comrades, my lawyer colleagues; it's almost like an ache. I long for news of how they are coping. My biggest purchase from the Canteen is always notebooks and pens. I meticulously make brief notes on the news items that interest me: news of workers' struggles, talk of new labour codes; land and displacement issues, poverty and inequality; the latest judgments and gossip about courts and judges. And of course . . . anything and everything to do with my home state, Chhattisgarh. Why? After all, I know I will never read those notes again. Perhaps it is my little act of protest, of stubbornness. To say no, I will not be cut off, I refuse to be cut off, my knowing all this still matters, I will live to fight another day.

One day there is a news item on the Report of the Judicial Enquiry Commission into the Sarkeguda 'encounter'. Sarkeguda is a village deep inside the Bijapur district of the Bastar region in Chhattisgarh. The villagers have been vindicated as the Commission has concluded that the seventeen villagers killed by security forces in June 2012 were not 'dreaded Maoists' but ordinary unarmed villagers, including six minors. Vivid memories rush to my mind as I recall listening to their families' heart-rending stories, marvelling at the courage of the young nurse who leads them and translates their Gondi into Hindi. I remember typing out their affidavits and the difficult search for a notary brave enough to put his stamp on the papers. I remember the bedraggled group appearing before the Secretary to the Commission after a night-long bus journey, the arguments with a snooty bureaucratic clerk to extend the time for the submission of their affidavits and the gruff voice of the judge heading the Commission on the telephone: 'Madam, rest assured, my job is to uncover the truth, not to conceal it. My office will accept the affidavits.' Later, a brave group of women lawyers based in Bastar was to represent the case of the villagers before the Commission. But the irony – on the day they are vindicated, seven years after they began their fight, I, their first lawyer, am in a jail 1,000 kilometres away! Yet it is a happy day.

Winter has come around again. This year it is really cold. I am bathing and washing my clothes on alternate days to make judicious use of the four buckets of water that I can store in my cell. The very cold water is quite invigorating after the first mugful hits you with a shock. We have to ask permission from our Madams on guard to dry our clothes in the patch of sun on the Stage, because otherwise they will take forever to dry. Shoma Di patiently waits till the afternoon bandi when one of the Madams can escort her to the solar heater to get half a bucket of hot water to ease the pain in her knees. Our neighbours of course try their best to hog as much hot water as they can and grudge her even her half bucket. The Madams chose diplomatically to pander to their pressure. Whatever momentous things might be happening in the outside world, the mundane daily struggle of our existence in jail goes on unabated . . .

61

I have been avoiding writing about her, this prisoner who shares the Phansi Yard with us, but now it's probably time to do so. She is in her mid-forties – a strong, portly, 'wheatish'-complexioned woman, with thinning hair and two broken front teeth (witnesses to the many fights she has got into). She and her thinner, taller younger sister have been in jail for more than twenty-three years now, nearly eighteen of them in isolation in this Phansi Yard. They and their mother were in and out of jail in their childhood for petty thefts. It is not clear whether they are sonars (goldsmiths) as she claims, or belong to the denotified or scheduled tribes community. They have been accused of kidnapping and murdering some thirteen children. Their mother was also an accused and has died during the pendency of the case. The case in its time caused a sensation and was given to the ever-crusading Maharashtra prosecutor Ujwal Nikam. He wanted the death penalty at any cost for the 'crazy sisters', and he got it.

From her story, one thing is clear. The sisters and their mother were no doubt the lesser mercenaries in a sordid chain of crime, but not the kingpins. According to her, there was a gory nexus of petty criminals and hospital staff carrying out trafficking and organ sales. More than a hundred women and children were first trafficked into prostitution and then shifted to hospitals. Some of them had their organs 'harvested', and some of them were also killed and their bodies disposed of. Children were trafficked abroad . . . She has the details of hospitals involved – they are well-established places. It was not a crime that three barely literate women could have possibly committed by themselves.

The man who has turned approver in her case, her husband's brother, is one of the lynchpins, she says. Let's call him X. So the story she tells is that X was working as a driver for two well-off women deep into trafficking. Then the tentacles spread to organ sale. It appears that the role of our yard-mates, while despicable, was limited to the snatching of kids and keeping them for a day or two till the 'plans' kicked in. She says her husband had come to know of some crores of cash stashed away by X in various places. She and her husband had found this money, concealed it by redistributing it, and subsequently both brothers fought over it. Her husband was murdered in front of her eyes by X. So, in this strange way, she is both victim and co-conspirator.

Later, X had tried to get her to reveal the whereabouts of the money she and her husband had stashed away. It was because she refused, in her stupid street-smart way, that he finally testified against the two sisters before the court, blaming them for the murders. His is the only direct evidence against the two of them. The bodies of most of the kidnapped children were never found. And in one case a family refused to acknowledge a child as their missing child, and the DNA didn't match either.

The death sentence of the two sisters was subsequently stayed, and the final hearing keeps being adjourned. Any which way, they are stuck here forever, for the alternative to the death penalty is, in this case of multiple murders, forty years of imprisonment. Meanwhile, the larger criminal machinery of trafficking and organ sale remains untouched.

When she came to jail, she was around twenty-five, with four sons – the eldest about seven and the youngest some eight months old. Her younger sister was just nineteen. The children were all taken away from her and put in a sanstha. She had to fight a long custody battle from jail to prove they were her own. When she came to this jail, there weren't even toilets in the Yard – one had to shit in an earthen pot, the kunda, which was emptied or disposed of by manual scavengers.

Over this period of time, the sisters have become the most hated and feared prisoners here. She has a really foul tongue and gets worked up and infuriated on the slightest pretext. When angry, she lets out a continuous torrent of abuse at the Constables or other prisoners. She has been known to smash toilets, throw her food umpteen times outside her cell and even hurl soiled menstrual cloths at the Constables. She has been violent with other prisoners in the Phansi Yard. I sometimes feel sorry for the younger sister, who is in her shadow. She does not always approve of the things her sister does and sometimes makes feeble efforts to shake off her influence, but ends up being her slave, echoing her obnoxious allegations.

Over time, the rules have been relaxed a little and they are now allowed out of their cells into the corridor and permitted to roll out agarbattis in their corner of the Phansi Yard. But woe betide any prisoner even mistakenly combing her hair or drying her clothes or spitting in the area around their corner of our 'cage', and the abuse begins.

Having been around her for a year now, I have to grudgingly

appreciate the fight she puts up continually with the authorities for small concessions – to be allowed out for an hour, to have a proper calculation of her wages, to get the proper measure of milk or tea. But there is also her personal egotism, her obsession to dominate and her absolute selfishness, even vis-à-vis her sister. She can't bear being ordered around or to play second fiddle. Of late her attention is focused on showing Shoma Di and me who is boss in the Yard. She has done this with all the previous occupants of these cells too. She keeps coming up with excuses to fight with us, complain against us – we are talking to another prisoner, we are using too much water, we talk too loudly, we whisper to each other. So she abuses and occasionally threatens us, which is quite stupid, considering that we are actually relatively sympathetic and helpful. I have even helped her communicate with a better lawyer. But that's how she has probably been all her life – penny-wise and pound-bloody-foolish!!

Cats

I remember how shocked I was the night I came in last year by the sudden appearance of a ginger tabby with a huge furry tail as I put on my clothes in the dim light of the jhadti room next to the Gate. Now he is a familiar sight. His name is Shankar, but we have nicknamed him Bhishma Pitamah since he seems to be the sire of half a dozen other ginger cats and kittens of various generations and sizes. Then there is a mangy-looking black tabby, the local goonda, who comes in to fight and compete on Shankar's territory. There are two or three mature females who wander around the whole jail – their favourite place being around the BC, of course, but also in the grounds and barracks, picking off scraps of spilled food, snapping up insects, rats, lizards and some unlucky birds. And having litters of three or four kittens every few months.

Cats are a boon, particularly for us in isolation – the only creatures who can step freely in and out of the bars of the Yard. Watching the kittens blink their eyes, mew demandingly, catch their tails, roll over and box each other, clean their faces with their tiny paws, climb and slip down trees, stretch luxuriously in the most complicated yoga poses, fluff up and snooze in the winter sun, is one of the joys of prison life.

Surprisingly, our yard-mates are very fond of kittens. In the past year we have seen two batches of kittens grow up in the Yard and then gradually migrate, die or be removed in a sack and left in the Open Jail fields. I had a good time watching and playing with the first lot who really made jail life so much more human. But their 'owners', the sisters, have grown extra possessive, so I'm consciously keeping a distance from the second lot.

Through the bars of the Yard I watch a pregnant cat, Sonu, following the Warder of the BC around, hoping to get a bit of the breakfast milk that's bound to be spilt when it is served, or perhaps even having some milk offered to her by a kindly prisoner. One day she carries one of her weaker kittens across the jail and climbs on the roof of Barrack No. 2 and puts it into an abandoned water tank for safety. Then suddenly the cover of the tank clangs shut and she is unable to get the kitten out. The entire jail watches open-mouthed a day later, when a brave young prisoner climbs up to the roof to the water tank and triumphantly gets out the continuously mewing, starving little kitten.

We hear with awe that Shankar has killed a snake in the jail's lobby, the Gate (these reptiles are very much a part of jail life). Often the silence of the nights is pierced by the loud mating cries of cats, like those of wailing children, or the snarls and roars of their territorial fights.

Sundays

No prisoner loves Sundays, because that's the day we are locked in at 2 p.m. instead of 5 p.m. For us in isolation, it means we get to spend only around five out of twenty-four hours in the corridor outside our individual cells, where Shoma Di and I can talk to each other, eat together and be closer to the life outside the Yard. Still, Sundays do feel different.

The Factory is closed on Sunday, and visits to the Open Jail (fields) are often suspended, so there is a sense of leisure for those who do regular work. We get suji halwa for breakfast on Sundays and kadhi or besan for lunch. A pouch of shampoo is distributed on three out of four Sundays. The afternoon bandi is an hour earlier, at 11 a.m., and lasts till 1 p.m., and our dinner arrives at 2 p.m, which of course has to be kept carefully aside to be consumed later.

Sundays also feel different because of the washing of the barracks turn by turn. All the bags and bedrolls and bundles and bottles are kept on the Stage or in the Hall, while whosoever's turn it is (three or four of the inmates of that particular barrack) bring tins of water on their heads from the hauz in the common bathing sheds or from various drums and Sintex tanks kept in different corners of the campus. Others scrub the floor, sweep away the water or swab the floor dry in the barracks and corridors.

Sunday is also the day many of the convicts get to phone home (*this is a pre-Covid account*), unlike undertrials who are not provided this facility. A Constable sits with the token-operated telephone and a fat register on a stool in front of her, recording names and numbers. Often one of the Warders helps with the dialling and noting down of numbers. The women sit around in the Hall and on the steps awaiting their turn. Sometimes there are happy sounds – some relative has got married or has had a kid or someone is coming for a mulakat. At other times there are loud wails – someone has died or is very ill. Sometimes it's complicated – the person at the other end doesn't have a phone and has to be called to one – at such times the Constable may also use her personal phone. Or even wait for a call back. This is the only time that a Constable is allowed to carry her phone into the jail instead of depositing it at the Gate. As with everything else in jail, there is no concept of privacy. Everybody sits around the person on the phone, giving instructions like, 'Say this'... or 'Hurry up'.

The last Sunday of the month is special. That's the day women prisoners go to meet their relatives in the Main Jail – husbands, fathers, brothers, sons; but only 'legal relatives' – not boyfriends, or friends or co-accused. Children are dressed carefully to meet their fathers. The women also comb their hair and dress up more than usual. The jail van usually makes three trips, carrying twelve to fifteen prisoners each time. Earlier, I hear, families could meet face to face, and fathers could hug their children. But, as everywhere else, 'security has been tightened' with regard to these meetings too. So, this visit happens across a glass pane and through a phone line, but it is a visit nevertheless.

62

One of the Warders is telling a 'funny' story and the prisoners listening are guffawing in merriment. We are waiting to receive our canteen, which she is distributing. She is the Warder of Barrack No. 3 in which most of the undertrials are housed. She is talking about a Sindhi mother and daughter who have been here a few weeks now. They both look very genteel and soft; very middle class, and speaking Hindi in an anglicized manner. The mother is shorter, bespectacled, with her grey hair in a ponytail. The daughter is taller and quite beautiful, with her silky hair done up in a bun. They both wear cotton churidar-kurtas. The two women and the girl's father have apparently been arrested for fraudulent bank transactions. I am surprised to hear that they had been here earlier too.

Anyway, to come to the 'story'. The daughter has a fungal infection around her thighs and between her legs. She needs to use the common bathroom to wash the affected area with Dettol soap in the mornings. But her other barrack-mates don't want to accommodate her and are too smart for her.

One after the other they pretend they need to go to the loo urgently so that her turn never comes.

She gets very frustrated and complains to the Warder, 'Tai, they abuse me in Marathi.' 'So you abuse them back,' the Warder replies. 'But I don't know any abuses,' she says helplessly. 'Okay, I will teach you,' the Warder says. 'Say *chhinaal* [whore].' The Warder is in splits of laughter as she describes the way the girl shouts '*cheenaal*' in her odd accent at the other women and pushes her way into the bathroom. Perhaps hers is the inverted snobbery of the underdog class, or just sheer appreciation of the way this greenhouse plant has adapted to the jungle!

(As an aside, fungal infections are very common in jails. This is because of the shared bathrooms, toilets and overcrowded barracks. Like so many others, I developed a very persistent fungal infection in Byculla Jail, which I attribute to the fact that we would dry our clothes on the stone floor of our courtyard during the afternoon bandi *– the only place there would be sun. This floor used to be washed each morning with stinking municipal water that was probably contaminated. Anyway, being a diabetic I am more prone to infections and am a very slow healer. So more than a year after my release, I am still struggling with the infection, which recurs as soon as medication stops.)*

63

And one day we hear a not-at-all funny story, in fact a horrid story, about a convict who was released a few months back.

Her husband had abducted a minor girl and raped her for three days. It seems she sat on a chair outside her house and prevented the mohalla people from entering it. The man absconded. Her face was blackened and she was paraded naked through the mohalla. When she was brought to jail she used to be terrified of people and recovered only gradually. Eventually her husband was caught and they were both convicted. He was a smart and shrewd fellow. He became a Warder in the Main Jail, then a Canteen-in-Charge and finally went to the Open Jail and was released a couple of years before she was. As in life, so in jail, she paid for his misdeeds and had the worse deal.

64

We've seen her progress slowly towards her death. She begins by suffering from uncontrollable diarrhoea. The kundewali complains bitterly, 'Oh, she still eats mangoes and has dahi . . . just doesn't listen . . . and then soils her bedding.' She has to be bathed and her bedding washed every now and then. Our Constable remarks, 'The kundewali only complains, but which daughter-in-law would do as much?' One day, she crosses our Phansi Yard, supported by a young girl. She is being brought back from the toilet completely naked . . . It is a terrifying sight – her frail, pale body with bedsores over her buttocks . . . Our yard-mates start a torrent of abuse. 'The so-and-so!! She has spoilt our roza (mind you, they are not Muslims but observe roza). Such a sight. May maggots devour her ...' That's the last time she goes past our Yard.

Then start the trips to Sassoon Hospital. A couple of times we see her being helped to walk slowly to the Gate in her nightie, normally an absolute no-no, but they have given up on saris for her now. On one occasion she soils her nightie before she even gets to the Gate and has to be brought back to the barrack. Each time she is admitted to hospital, the prisoners in the Hospital Barrack, where she is housed, breathe easy. 'Where's your mother-in-law?' the Constables tease the kundewali. The Constable who had admitted her to hospital says the old woman refused to let go of her hand until another familiar Constable took over. 'She told me the doctor had told her son she has only a few months to live.' But after a few days on saline, she is back in jail.

Now they start taking her to Aundh, a Pune locality. This is the place where a medical board will certify her release on the basis of old age and long incarceration. She needs a wheelchair, can't walk any more. One day, in the Saturday Round, the Jail Superintendent does the unthinkable. He actually steps into the Hospital Barrack to see her. Normally the inmates all line up outside, but now she can't even get up. The last time she goes to Sassoon Hospital, she is carried by four women in a ghongri. She has lost the use of her arms and legs now. Finally, her release order and her surprisingly well-to-do son both arrive. It's a relief to see her leave the jail alive, even if as a bundle, feet first.

65

A new pair has come to the Hospital Barrack – mother and daughter – convicted for ten years under the PITA and POCSO Acts. They were undertrials in the Beed District Jail and have come here after being convicted. Unlike most other PITA undertrials or convicts, they are not urban-based or Bengali/Nepali, but seem to be from a local rural background. The mother looks in her fifties, with unruly grey hair. She wears her sari like old rural women do, just below the knees, and she hobbles to and fro. The daughter is in her thirties and has only one leg. The other is a stump at the thigh. She lost a leg when a truck went over it when she was just five years old. She supports herself expertly with a crutch. She has been given salwar-kurtas to wear. She's thin and the ends of her hair tied up in a ponytail are a golden brown – she must have dyed them that way before she was convicted. Her thin, dark face has many pockmarks. She is married and has a daughter, who is five now and lives with her sister. I hear her husband has abandoned her now and remarried.

The mother and daughter claim that the two minor girls found with them had been left with them by someone who asked them to look after the girls. But the villagers have complained of trafficking on their part. In the poor rural backwaters of drought-prone Beed district, there might well be such trafficking. But if this is the socio-economic condition of the 'Madams' who benefit from such trafficking, it must be a pretty sad business. And where and who are the 'customers'? As usual, they have got away.

66

They are as different from each other as cheese from chalk, and yet have something in common, for they have both been arrested for their absconding husbands' crimes and are both mothers of small children. They are classic 'judicial hostages', hauled into prison while the man in their lives evades justice. Let me call them A and B.

A is petite and looks like a typical middle-class upper-caste Maharashtrian with her neat synthetic sari, her cultured speech and fine features. She is held under MCOCA. Her absconding husband is alleged to have been involved in gang robberies, and unfortunately for her the properties he bought with his ill-gotten gains are in her name. She says she knew very little about her husband's activities and went into a state of shock when she was called to the police station and confronted with three other women – all purportedly 'wives' her husband had in different cities. Her pretty, talkative daughter is the darling of the Bais. She walks around the jail holding the finger of one of them and reciting nursery rhymes coquettishly, like a parrot. She is nearly four now and has begun going to the jail nursery school just outside the jail campus with the elder kids. But I never see the mother and daughter go to court – possibly the trial will not commence till the main accused is arrested? Also, in MCOCA cases, they need a special armed guard and an officer of at least sub-inspector rank, even for the accused to be taken to court.

B has Bengali features and sharp canines that make her look somewhat witch-like. She seems a little mentally deficient and speaks incessantly when she starts up. We encounter her in the court lock-up while we wait to be called to court for our case. When she's brought in she's really angry. 'Look at that Constable! She's demanding Rs 2,000 from me to get something to eat for my child. My sister had come and she didn't even let me talk to her!' The Constable, when she locks her in, sees all of us sharing some food another prisoner has got from home (no doubt after paying an appropriate bribe). The Constable snaps, 'Hey, don't let that woman eat anything. Don't give anything to her . . .'

B's son is so different from her – fair with curly golden-brown hair, a cute little boy just learning to lisp a few words. Looking at the incongruous mother-and-son pair, an unkind thought occurs to me – that the child's father has probably used her and then abandoned her. He seems to be charged with gangsterism and is absconding. She readily concurs, 'Oh, his papa, pah, he just left us in this mess and ran away . . .'

67

Many women here are from families and neighbourhoods where 'number 2 ka dhandha' (some illegal business) is a way of life. This is the parallel petty-crime economy, widespread in the underbelly of urban life, with its deep nexus with the police, local officials, gangsters and corporators.

I meet a pretty young woman of the Mang community here. She says she had a boyfriend from her locality who was a pickpocket. But she didn't feel secure being with someone like that, and they drifted apart. Then the young man she is now married to, a smart Maratha with a flourishing 'number 2 ka dhandha' (she doesn't specify what it is) fell madly in love with her. They have been married several years now and she has two daughters. She describes how he pampers her. She is the only woman in his immediate family – her mother-in-law has died, her husband has no sisters and her younger brother-in-law is unmarried. Yet she never has to cook! In fact, for many years they all used to eat at her mother's place, which is just a couple of houses away. 'In my house, my mother and bhabhis cook for all of them, and for all of us too, and for all the "boys in the business". They use up five kilos of atta for each meal.'

In the course of time, her husband got involved in some serious 'business conflict' and has now been jailed for murder. After that her ex-boyfriend began harassing her, stalking her and even threatened to throw acid on her. By this time he was himself married, with children, but that didn't stop him from trying to force her into a relationship with him. Her husband, she says, was aware of this earlier relationship when he married her. (In fact, he seems to be remarkably philosophical about pre-marital relationships – 'Oh, everyone has them,' she claims he said.) One day, during a mulakat, she told her husband that she was getting seriously threatened and harassed, and he said, 'Finish him off.' She seems to have taken his advice seriously, since she is in jail on a murder charge. 'I am waiting for him to "manage" his case and get out. Then he will "manage" mine!' she says confidently. This 'other' world, where murder and bribery and hafta and number 2 ka dhandha are so casually talked about, has been quite an eye-opener for me.

One day, on the way back from court, after being bullied by the police and not being allowed to meet my young women associates who had come all the way from Chhattisgarh, I am surprised to see an otherwise stern woman police Guard getting biryani and samosas for this young prisoner. She has to eat sitting crouched on the floor of the police van as we return so that she is not visible. Her husband had also been brought to court for his case, and they were permitted to meet. This young woman is allowed to use the Constable's phone to talk to her mother and hint, within earshot of everyone, that 'another thousand is due'.

I am always struck by how different the world of 'political crime' is from the world of 'regular crime'. Political cases are dealt with such sternness and inflexibility, but in the case of regular crime, everything from food in the lock-up to favourable court orders seem to be manageable for a price.

'House-peeking' and other 'trainings'

No, that is not a spelling mistake. These days an NGO is conducting 'housekeeping' training in jail, but it is referred to by almost everybody as 'house-peeking'. Two fat and lazy-looking ladies come to the Hall to teach, with some prisoners in tow carrying yellow-handled mops, brooms, chequered dusters, trays of Colin glass cleaner and other paraphernalia. A good number of undertrials have signed up. Opinion is divided among the onlookers. One set feels: 'What's the use of teaching women to clean? They do it anyway, and much better than with all this newfangled stuff!' The other lot point out: 'But this is for employment in malls and hotels and hospitals. Getting even such jobs is not easy. Does the NGO organize jobs too?' That part is true. It's not easy for a convict or even an undertrial to get a job, even the most informal one. Anyway, there they all are, practising mopping the Stage and corridors while others look on with a mixture of curiosity and amusement. Soon, the ten-day long training is done and all the NGO ladies have been felicitated with bouquets.

Many such 'trainings' keep taking place in the Women's Jail. The longest-running one is the 'parlour course', in which the prisoners have been given some fancy manuals and are being taught to do threading, facials, etc. One of our kundewalis, who is doing the course and likes playing the joker, says, 'Oh I can't say all those English names – 'message' (massage) and 'fesal' (facial) – so they laugh at me. And whom do I practise the "eyebrows" on? The old women in the Hospital Barrack?'

Sometimes there is a three-to-five-day mehndi course, where intricate designs are drawn first on paper and then on each other's hands. The classes are conducted by a serious-looking lady, who comes with charts of complicated designs and mock-mehndi cones of paint. There is also a rakhi training on at the moment. After the training is done, many of the convicts and undertrials will be employed in the jail factory to make rakhis for the Jail Showroom. Of course, they will be paid peanuts.

All these training courses are supervised by the two social workers at the Women's Jail and Teacher Madam. The social workers are also supposed to visit the homes of prisoners and the children placed in sansthas. They are, in fact, meant to be the lifeline of the prisoners with the outside world, but seem distant, harassed and involved in paperwork all the time. One of them, after weeks of requesting on the Round, and several applications, has finally visited the children of our co-prisoners in the Phansi Yard. She contacted them through the police station of the area where their address is located, and they were understandably terrified by this police enquiry. However, she did finally visit their home and asked them to visit their mother, which they had not done for more than a year. While passing the bars of the Yard, she tells us she wants to do a PhD on the psychosocial background of the prisoners. When we enthusiastically encourage her, she complains, 'But we never get any time!!' We want to tell her that all she needs to do is to keep her eyes and ears open at work and reflect on the lives of the people she is surrounded by all the time. Doesn't she have the time to do that?

Below the surface

We are alarmed to learn from our male co-accused on a court date that there has been a communal clash in the Main Jail. A Muslim prisoner has been taken to the ICU in Sassoon Hospital, badly injured, including in the face. Apparently, this incident began with some Muslim prisoners attacking non-Muslims. Soon afterwards there was organized retaliation. The beatings, ironically, took place in Gandhi Yard and the sounds were clearly audible in the cells where our co-accused are lodged. It seems, from what we have heard, that the seniormost jail authorities gave a tacit go-ahead to the retaliation. Such news one only hears by word of mouth. 'Bad news' about any jail is carefully cut out from our newspapers. Even a murder in a Punjab jail was cut out.

We see the DIG Madam a week later, at the performance of an iconic Marathi folk play, *Gadhvache Lagna* (Marriage of the Donkey) in the Women's Jail. It is a hilarious play, where a kumbhar (potter) cocks a snook at 'gods', 'rajas' and 'dewans', a typical tongue-in-cheek take-down of feudal practices. The play is improvised and full of sexual innuendoes, which sometimes escape me but keep the audience in splits. During the bonhomie and the inevitable bouquets and exaggerated praise showered on our chief guests – the jail authorities – a chill goes down my spine when I think about what lies below this pleasant surface: the communalization of the top brass and what implications for the future that might hold.

A happier postscript: A month later, the Muslim wife and the Hindu girlfriend of the injured Muslim gangster are sitting together outside Barrack No. 2. They have put their heads together and are discussing with great concern whether he was looking better or not in the videoconference mulakat he had with his wife.

68

A prisoner, her mother-in-law and their male co-accused – her husband, her jeth, and father-in-law in the Main Jail –

have all taken a transfer to Nashik Jail. We will miss this young woman, a short, bouncy creature with a round, smiling face and a thick black plait, moving around the jail, mostly carrying jugs of tea and glasses to serve the Constables. She used to work in the BC and was universally liked and called by a loving nickname. She had been married for just fifteen days when she was arrested, along with her husband and other in-laws. Her jethani (jeth's wife) had committed suicide. Apparently there was some conflict and jealousy around this latest marriage – dowry perhaps, or the better looks or background of the new bride.

This is a common story in jail. Entire families are picked up on the death of the daughter-in-law, including in this case, a bride of a mere fifteen days. How could this very new entrant into the family have been part of a 'conspiracy of abetment to suicide'? I am shocked by the sheer unreasonableness of it.

Indian criminal law was amended because of the demands of women's movements to make it possible to prosecute brutal harassment behind closed doors, to which there were no witnesses. This was an important and necessary step, but in the practice of a corrupt and patriarchal police, it has often led to women of the marital family being arrested even when evidence against them is scant. In this case, the men have also been arrested, but there are so many cases where only the women are picked up. I have talked about some of these cases earlier here.

Besides, this 'overkill' in response to the death of daughters-in-law is complemented by absolute apathy and systemic indifference to the countless complaints of beating, torture and harassment by living daughters-in-law! Surely, prevention should be more important than retribution.

69

I am impressed by her pleasant, smiling face, her neatness and efficiency and the impression she gives of being educated. She used to be a bus conductor, and it is easy to imagine her in a conductor's khaki overshirt, snapping tickets efficiently and counting out change to the passengers. She and her mother regularly attend the Om Shanti sermons. She reads out the typed sermons on Sundays and other days when the Brahma Kumaris don't come to the jail. Both she and her mother work – she in the Minda factory, wearing her white coat, and her mother in the BC. I often see her mother carrying the large aluminium vessel of breakfast food on her head to the barracks, where it is placed before the gates are opened at 7 a.m.

I find that this prisoner has an interest in politics too. She criticizes the government when she hears, as we wait for the mulakat together, that ours is a 'political' case. I think to myself, this is one of the things that participating in public employment and economic life does to women – it helps them make much greater sense of the world outside the four walls of their home. The greatest loss to her family has been that of her government job. Her brother has come to visit her and her mother. 'I am lucky. He looks after my children and takes care of both of us,' she remarks, as always, with a smile. Later I come to know that they are convicted for life for the death of her bhabhi . . . Questions dart through my mind, and I have no answers to them: The wife of this very brother? Or another one?

70

She is a tall, gawky creature with a weather-beaten rural woman's face and mehndi-dyed hair. I'm guessing she is in her early fifties or so. We've seen her go from an undertrial to a convict. I remember the day, in the court lock-up, when she was brought in after the last bit of evidence was adduced. She was extremely tense and tearful. 'What happened?' 'Did the evidence go badly?' 'What does the lawyer say?' Everyone is bombarding her with questions. She just nods speechlessly. The witnesses have all testified against them. Their lawyer is saying, 'It's difficult now.' Suddenly, from the bars of the lock-up, she sees her husband and two sons being escorted back to their jail van in handcuffs. '*Jeva, Jeva!*' (Eat, eat, don't be upset), she shouts to them. A mother to the last moment.

I hear later that she has been sentenced to a double life term. A land dispute between their family and another family in the village had turned violent. Two people were killed by 'their side'. But barring a short period after her sentence, when she looked very depressed and seemed not to be eating or bathing as usual, I have always seen this woman talking loudly in her typical rural accent – joking, laughing and working, always working. Sweeping the roads and the maidan with a large broom, helping prepare the flower beds, or plastering mud and cow dung on the brick platforms around the trees for prisoners to sit on. A lot of her time is now taken up by another prisoner's little toddler, for whom she is his adopted 'grandmother'. 'Aayi' (Mother!) he calls her loudly – sometimes even grandmas are called that. After 'Mumma' and 'Bai' for the Constables, this is the third word in his limited vocabulary. If she doesn't pick him up and put him on her hip as she goes around, there will be loud bawling and wringing of hands and stomping of feet from the little fellow. And she loves to tease him.

The toilet is choked!

The toilet in Barrack No. 1 has got choked. Everyone grumbles at the anonymous bayka (women) who are always blamed when anything goes wrong. 'Someone must have thrown in a napkin. Or a plastic bag. Or a mug. Or shampoo pouches.' It never seems to occur to the people in charge that when there is one loo shared by some forty or often more barrack-mates on an average, it is bound to get choked some time. And indeed, one by one, nearly all the barrack toilets have got choked over my time here. The problem is that the repairs take up to ten and fifteen days. The PWD guys have to come in and clean the entire pipeline. In the meanwhile there is an awful stench. The very first day, most of the women of that barrack are shifted out to other barracks – No. 2 or 3 or 4 or the Hospital Barrack. And then all the fun and games begin.

The women are loathe to leave their barrack, even if there

is inconvenience, stench or threat of illness, particularly the long-standing convicts, for whom their little corner of a barrack has become home. Having neighbours you have come to an equilibrium with, as you sleep on your strip of the floor and they sleep on either side of you, is also very important. Being shifted to a new place seems a huge misery, even if the problems are the same everywhere. 'There are so many mosquitoes there!' (And not here?) 'It's too crowded' (And here?) Some of them have slyly made their way back. Some beg and plead with the more soft-hearted Senior Constables and, taking their exasperation for acquiescence, have triumphantly re-ensconced themselves. The smart, authoritative Warder is furious. There is a big fight with one of the old convicts – a very manly old woman. The Warder has apparently kicked her, and she begins to wail. The entire barrack gets a sharp talking-to at bandi time, and there are wholesale shifts. 'According to the Rules, you are to be shifted every month,' says Jailer Madam, 'and no one is to disobey.' So suddenly there are a whole lot of undertrials in their coloured civvies in Barracks 1 and 2 (traditionally the Convict Compound) and the long-standing green-saried convicts are migrating to Barracks 3 and 4 in the Undertrial Compound. Actually, the bathing and water facilities are better in the Undertrial Compound, but the convicts are furious.

The next morning there is tension again. This time a small group of undertrials who have been shifted to Barrack No. 2 have refused to take their bhatta. In any case, there has been enormous confusion in the distribution of bhatta – with numbers in some barracks having expanded and in others having contracted sharply. But hunger strike is a jail offence, a revolt. So, the entire Barrack No. 2 is brought to the Hall. Jailer Madam strides in purposefully in an I-will-not-brook-any-nonsense mood. Someone is crying and there are raised voices. Then we hear Madam – 'If you have a problem, make an application. I will send it to your court, but here you have to abide by the discipline.' After a short while everyone troops out. The Warder shouts – 'This is the last time I'm telling all of you – go and get your bhatta.' The knot of rebels is disintegrating. Slowly they go to the BC with their plates and katoris. One of the kundewalis – a tall, plump and talkative personality – has come across to them. One of the 'rebels' is her maushi's daughter. She has taken the crying girl aside and is counselling her, persuading her to be calm and get her food. Eventually she succeeds in sending her to the BC.

Of course, the main cause of all the ruckus – the toilet – remains choked.

71

A new admission has come in – a youngish woman in a salwar-kurta and ponytail. She can be heard loudly wailing all through the night. In the morning we see her screaming even more loudly at the Gate, insisting on being let out. 'I want to go home to my Mummy and Papa!' There are mixed reactions. 'Hey! She seems to be a bit cracked in the head!' 'Oh! It's all a drama!' 'If one could get bail just by shouting, wouldn't we all be doing it too!' Apparently, she was caught entering someone's house. Already the jail grapevine has the information that this twenty-five-year-old has been married three times and abandoned each time. I am surprised that the mandatory medical examination after police custody and prior to judicial custody hasn't managed to locate the fault lines of what may well be a mental illness. While insanity is a defence in criminal law, there are so many types and degrees of mental ill health – intellectual disability, violent behaviour, personality disorder, claustrophobia, schizophrenia and even kleptomania – that need to be taken into account.

After some talking-to by the Jailer Madam, she sits quietly for an hour or so under the peepal tree before making towards the Gate again. During bandi, she is locked in the barrack with the others and we hear her screaming loudly again. Sometime earlier, the prisoners who do duty as daily wagers at the Gate had tried, unsuccessfully, to take her to the doctor. She refuses food and only eats the biscuits someone offers. But it appears, finally, that she has somehow been administered a sedative. All's quiet at night. One prisoner remarks, 'If she's acting up, she'll "get it" in the Mental Hospital. They give electric shocks and beat people. Better to be here . . .'

72

This young and so obviously Bengali Muslim woman, despite her smile, has big brown eyes ready to fill up with tears. She sits next to me for a dance programme, which we have been specially allowed to attend. While we wait for the troupe to arrive, the jail kids are putting up a remarkably good impromptu show on the Stage. As I turn to her, expressing appreciation for the children, she starts wiping her eyes. 'My children are this age too.' Hers is the simplest of crimes, if it is a crime at all. She doesn't have a passport and is facing prosecution along with her husband as an illegal migrant. She's not the right religion, you see. I don't have the heart to ask her where her children are.

There are many Bangladeshi women here. Some serve terms and are escorted to the border and handed over to the Bangladesh Border Police. Others have been able to get Aadhaar cards made, so it's additionally a complicated case of possession of fraudulent documents. The Hindu migrants are luckier. With all that we are reading in the news about the Citizenship Amendment Bill and National Register of Citizens and the threats of establishing Foreigners Tribunals in all the states, I feel frightened. There are the Sri Lankan Tamils (including a large number of Christians) in Tamil Nadu, Pakistani herdsmen and fishermen in Rajasthan, Tibetan refugees, Nepali chowkidars in Haryana and of course the Rohingyas, for whom the Government of India has thoughtfully constructed houses in Myanmar that the Rohingyas don't want to go back to because it's not safe . . . As history marches on and capital gets more and more globalized, there will be newer 'criminals' created and newer 'punishments' meted out. People just trying to survive, just trying to make ends meet, criss-crossing through elaborate trafficking networks over borders that have been drawn and redrawn in the common memory of three generations, will become 'dangerous criminals' for whom our Home Ministry will have 'no tolerance'. And yet we grumble when US visas become difficult and expensive for the educated youngsters of our elite who wish to study, work and settle abroad in their lakhs. Such NRIs are the 'jewels in our crown'. So unlike these, who are truly 'the wretched of the earth'.

73

Middle-class girls stick out in jail, and so does she, with hair that still looks conditioned in a shiny black ponytail, and her oversize glasses. We are told she was brought up in Dubai, spent the last two years in Kolkata and has been caught with (if newspaper accounts are to be believed) a surprisingly large amount of narcotics. The first day she sits outside the Mulakat Room in her jeans and top, looking very depressed and out of place. She doesn't speak Marathi, of course, and only a very anglicized Hindi in a Bengali tone. Actually, she doesn't even speak Bangla. We see her trying to settle in. She's quite scared even of the Tais, who scold her for not wearing a dupatta and for 'how short' her top is.

Some days later she breaks out in chickenpox and is brought to the Hospital Barrack, because the Undertrial Barracks are far too crowded and there are several children there. Her fever has subsided now and the scales have fallen from her pockmarks. On a day when it's her turn to bring the bhatta to the Hospital Barrack, we see her struggling to bring the sabzi in an aluminium drum with a very hot handle, and another day even carrying a bucket of water on her head.

'Hey! Can I talk to you? There's no one who can really understand me here,' she says one day as she passes the bars of our Phansi Yard, where Shoma Di and I are sitting in the corridor. She has heard about us while at Jadavpur University. Sad though it is, we have to tell her the rules. 'Sorry, no, you are not allowed to talk to us!' Casual conversation might still be ignored by the Constables on guard, but a heart-to-heart will certainly be objected to.

I wonder how she got herself into this mess? She doesn't seem to be suffering from any withdrawal symptoms or other signs of being an addict herself. Perhaps she got into the 'business' of selling or carrying drugs? Though her family does come to visit, she is clear-headed enough, I learn later, to realize that the sympathy might not last very long. Besides, the NDPS Act is a draconian law. Mere possession of drugs is a crime, nothing else needs to be proved, and ten-year sentences are fairly common. In her own way, she is a brave kid. I feel sorry for this mixed-up yet lovable generation.

74

She's really thin, with a birdlike face, large beady eyes, sharp nose, curly hair and a flashing smile of uneven teeth. She's sitting in the lock-up relating her story with gusto, interrupting it to regularly spit out tobacco in the far corner. She got married when she was thirteen, and it was an interreligious love marriage at that. She describes how, when she overheard talk of her being married off, she called her Hindu boyfriend and told him that this was the last time she was going to phone him. Next morning, when she went to answer nature's call at 4 a.m. (thank goodness there was no rule in place forbidding open defecation then), there he was, with a car. Her Muslim father searched for her and found her at her lover's house, where she had been accepted by his mother, a strong-minded only parent. When her father arrived, this lady apparently said, 'Yes, she is here. If she wants to go with you, you are welcome to take her.' The girl was called downstairs, where she sat demurely with her head covered and claims that she politely kept saying no. No, she wouldn't go home. No, not even until she became a major. No, not even for the preparations for marriage. And that was that.

Eventually, and it isn't clear how and why, her husband became a Muslim. When she became pregnant for the first time, her husband felt it was too early for them to have a child and wanted her to get an abortion, but her mother-in-law did not, and promised to look after the baby. She 'went on a strike', refused to even 'talk to' her husband (could be a euphemism for sexual activity) till he agreed to her having the baby. Now they have two children.

She was running a biggish dhaba (rustic hotel) with plenty of staff when she was arrested. She blames the manager she had appointed, saying he might have been doing some shady business on the side, thus getting her implicated in a PITA (prostitution) case. She says that when she was initially called to the police station and her father came there and was told by the police that it was a PITA case, he asked, 'What is it? Have you been stealing flour?' (In Marathi, flour is 'peeth'!) She openly swears violent revenge against that so-and-so (torrent of abuse) manager the moment she gets out on bail.

The next time I meet her is when we are both going down to Sassoon Hospital. I have some arthritic complaints. She has an enlarged gland near her throat, a severe stomach ache and is throwing up blood. She is remarkably calm though, and has fortunately stopped chewing tobacco. There's a need for blood tests and an ultrasound. For some reason she has been referred to the Surgery Department, even she does not know why. Two weeks later I see her, cheerful as ever, with her curly hair in a plait and flashing her bright smile. 'Haven't had the ultrasound yet, Aunty.'

75

A thin and brisk young mother is always the butt of criticism for neglecting her little boy. A cute two-year-old with a naughty look, a slight squint and a limited vocabulary of 'Bai', 'Tai', 'Mumma', most importantly 'Mau' (both for aunts [maushi] and cats [meow]) and a whole range of 'oohs' and 'aayees'. He is an energetic child, up early and perpetually getting in the way of everyone by playing at his favourite game – opening, closing and swinging the heavy barred iron gate of the barrack. His exploration of anything lying on the ground, including by tasting it, gets him hefty whacks from passing prisoners, and sometimes roars of laughter, such as when he prances around with a bra around his neck, which he had picked off a bush where it had been hung to dry. Of course, he can be cranky when he is ill and chooses the most inconvenient times to answer the call of nature. His mother, unfazed by all the scolding for neglecting him, is half a child herself, playing with him rather than taking care of him. She has come to jail in an NDPS case – found with some ten kilos of ganja, they say. Well, if it has been found in her possession, there isn't much to expect but a long sentence (unless all the talk of decriminalizing ganja materializes before her trial concludes). For her child, it would mean four more years in jail, and then separation from his mother.

76

She is a large, dark woman with a booming voice and a big teeka. She and her husband used to render all-night performances at villages, singing all the beautiful, rough-hewn traditional 'devi' songs dedicated to Kalubai, a form of Goddess Parvati specific to rural Maharashtra. In fact, we first notice her on one of the festival days, when she starts singing improvisations on life in jail as she sits on the Stage. At that time she was part of a group that had come from the Undertrial Compound, taking advantage of the little extra freedom that one gets on festival days to roam around the jail.

Nowadays she's in the Hospital Barrack. Being among the more able-bodied in her barrack, she often passes our Phansi Yard carrying the bhatta on her head. She always finds an excuse to sing a snippet of a song telling us what vegetable there is for lunch; or to give her exaggerated opinion of some jail happening as she passes by. Not that she is always pleasant. Being quite a 'fightercock', her arguments can be heard all over the jail.

She is in jail for having arranged the marriage of a minor. The girl ran away, and believe it or not, this prisoner is an accused under the Child Marriage Act. I think it's a joke – not because the girl was not a minor, of course she was, but because child marriage seems such a commonplace occurrence in the lives of the women in jail. Every second woman here was married as a minor. Anyway, the even bigger joke is that the girl (bride) who had run away with someone is also here now, apparently for being part of a robbery gang!

One can only watch this old maushi (as all the older women are referred to here) sway her hips and sing, 'Oh Kalubai!! You are the only Zandu Balm for the headaches of my life!', and wholeheartedly agree.

77

Among our African prisoners, apart from an elderly South African, who is now awaiting her release after completing her ten-year sentence, we now have two Ugandans. The elder looks like she is in her late twenties, though I realize our perception of age often misfires when it comes to another race. She is a large woman with big hips, large eyes and a flashing white smile. She usually wears long gowns and a knitted cap that covers her curly hair. After being introduced to us by the South African, whom the Ugandans naturally gravitated towards, she often greets us in a typical sing-song accent. The younger one is usually in long T-shirts and leggings. She is often running around filling buckets and bottles for the elder two. Whenever they get a chance, they sway their hips to music or, spotting a football, start throwing it to one another. They usually have a boiled vegetable diet with salads and also the 'extra medical diet' of boiled eggs and pavs. The three of them sit together on the raised platform around a tree eating their bhatta. The Senior Madam on duty that day has a funny relationship with them – half scolding, half joking – and now she shouts, 'Hey you three. Sit down on the ground and eat. You are not allowed to sit up there and eat!' She comes up to them and playfully slaps one on the shoulder. All of them smile at her, conveniently pretend not to understand what she is saying and carry on eating their food. Smart strategy.

Flying biryani

The lock-ups in the court are no better than the police lock-up I was first taken to. Dingy, unlit, with paan stains and dust and assorted kachra (rubbish) in the corners and the world's most undisturbed cobwebs hanging down, black with dust from the ceiling. There have been days when the lock-up smells terribly of a mix of phenyl and vomit, or else cat shit. Shoma Di makes a bit of noise on such a day, and we are shifted to a marginally better lock-up. Sometimes we are as many as twelve or fourteen women prisoners, some with babies too, all cooped up there. All the elderly are trying to get a place against the one clean wall to rest their aching backs. As soon as a case is called out in one of the courts, the Guards for that prisoner will come and escort her there.

One day, there are only the two of us remaining after everyone has been taken to court. Our case is usually called out at the very end. The voices from the men's section of the lock-up are always loud and raucous as groups of men, always handcuffed and strung along a long rope, are brought in and out from the jail vans, and to and from the courts. As we look through the bars of our cell in the lock-up barrack on to the enclosed courtyard of the lock-up compound with its peepal tree and a much-prayed-to god under it, suddenly we see a big bundle fly in from behind the outer wall studded with glass pieces. It's a big plastic bag full of what look like biryani packets. One of the Constables expertly fields it and quickly brings it into the lock-up barrack, bolting the gate from within, and goes towards the men's lock-up. Well, it seems some big dada has decided to treat all the prisoners (and of course, all the police Guards too) to biryani. Sometime later, the Constable, still munching, opens the barrack door, and the plastic bag with its empty foils, wrappers and cardboard boxes is on its outward journey by return flight across the wall. Whoosh! And that's a sixer!!

Epilogue

It's February 2020. The government in Maharashtra has changed. And the investigating agency in our case has changed too, from Pune Police to the National Investigation Agency. Now we shall be tried by the NIA Court at Mumbai and kept at the Byculla Women's Jail, part of the District Jail at Byculla, Mumbai. Shoma Di and I are 'packing'...

Our neighbours in the Phansi Yard have suddenly become pleasant. They ask for sweaters, extra buckets... It's easier to agree. Maybe they will miss us. We are taken to the godaam in the Hospital Barrack to get out our extra stuff accumulated over the year – like the clothes visitors gave us and we couldn't use because they exceeded our quota of two sets. All the old women prisoners are milling around curiously. 'Are you being released?' they ask hopefully. It's a tradition for those being released to distribute their old jail things, inauspicious to start a new life with. I give my socks, also not officially allowed in prison, and a scarf to a sick prisoner. We have already given away our current lot of books to our lawyers who came to visit. The enormous chargesheet has been tied up in a plastic sack. Shoma Di's commode chair is going too.

Finally, the jail van has come to transport us and we are escorted to the Gate amid many goodbyes. As usual the contents of our luggage are unceremoniously emptied out on the stone floor. By this time we are already on friendly terms with the Senior Women Constables and they wish us well ('Don't come back here again!') even as they go through our things and ruthlessly throw out precious objects – the occasional plastic spoon, the empty plastic boxes and Ziplock packets that we have ferreted away to store food in . . .

Then the bumpy ride in the van, with our bags and sack and chair, holding on to the side rails of the van for dear life when the driver suddenly decides to take off. After a long and hot road journey, we arrive at Byculla and enter a new set of enormous iron doors. For quite some time we stand uncertainly in the Gate area while the Guards and jail staff argue about various papers they don't seem to have . . . Then one more round of jhadti. The strip-search, the luggage check. Everything is thrown around all over again. Our medicines are taken away. 'You will only get them when our Jail Doctor approves.' Our precious Odomos tubes are thrown away ruthlessly. 'There are no mosquitoes here, we do regular fogging,' says the hard-faced slim young woman Guard checking our stuff. A young prisoner is called to help us carry our things to the Women's Circle – Circle No. 1 – an enclosed jail within the jail. As we stand in a corner of its small courtyard with high brick walls, feeling a little lost, we see the courtyard crammed with long queues for collecting the evening bhatta and a hundred pairs of curious eyes turned towards us . . . no doubt our reputation has preceded us.

Byculla is a whole new experience. An urban undertrial jail with no trees and gardens – at least for the women in our Circle. There are paths, tiny lawns, flower beds and potted plants outside our compound wall, but only the lucky male undertrials doing jail work like cooking or gardening or attending to the Canteen or Dispensary are allowed there. Ours is a two-storeyed building with six barracks and four separate cells. Here we are in ground-floor barracks. But Shoma Di and I end up in separate ones.

The barracks are long halls with one of the long sides made up of bars mounted on a shin-high ledge (so that the women can be watched at all times). There is a tiled bathing hall and four toilets attached to the barrack. It is lined with large drums for storing water, since water supply is for limited hours. The barrack and bathroom are lit up 24x7 with tubelights. When we enter for the first time, it's bewildering to see the large number of women with their bags and beddings and bottles and utensils stacked all along the four sides of the barrack and on the ledge. At night there will be pattis laid down, each touching the next, at right angles to all the walls, and two rows of pattis in the middle. The places are fixed by the Warder. Barrack No. 1 has all the new admissions for the first night, so after some squabbling we all somehow fit in. The next day I am shifted to Barrack No. 2.

In some ways, life in the barrack is more difficult – it is noisy and crowded, and we need to queue up for the toilets every morning. Each evening we obediently sit cross-legged in designated places for the Total – '302, NDPS, MCOCA (called Moka here), Mao, Naxal, Bengali UT, Bengali shiksha (convicted Bangladeshis), itar (all others)'. I am labelled 'Mao', and I raise my hand obediently when I hear the word. The women Constables shout out the numbers in each barrack as they move from barrack to barrack locking us in. When the prisoners in all the barracks have been counted – including the men in the Men's Jail – the Toll will sound. We are sleeping next to other prisoners in literally coffin-dimensioned spaces with our belongings stacked at our head, afraid to snore or turn too much in our sleep. But the isolation is broken, and we are with everyone else, to my great relief. For me, being among people is any day more comforting.

Everyday food, being cooked by the malc inmates, and with no home-grown vegetables and greens, is of a far poorer quality than at Yerawada – the sabzi is watery and too much masala floats in an unhealthily orange oil film on top. The rotis are sometimes burnt and at other times undercooked. Frankly, it depends on whether a good cook has been arrested or not, we joke. Fortunately, the dal and rice are quite sufficient, both in quantity and quality. And this being an undertrial jail, almost every Sunday we get 'specials', probably because that is one of the ways of preventing many better-off prisoners from making applications for home food to which they may be theoretically entitled. Specials include chicken, chana masala, and even the occasional noodles or vada pav. Of course, this is only for the ones who can afford to sign for it out of their PPC account, but eventually it does get distributed around. As in Yerawada, the poor are willing to do the barrack duties of the better off for a bit of Canteen/special food. While that is largely the trade-off, it is not always so. One very well-to-do Muslim lady in our barrack makes it a habit of ordering large quantities of non-veg specials for charitable purposes, and on those days there is a whole line of indigent prisoners queueing up at our barrack door with their katoris, waiting to be dished out some. (Don't ask how she manages this within her PPC allowance – it's one of those open secrets.)

Unlike Yerawada, there is just one NGO coming to the jail and hardly any 'trainings', but the women have their ways of devising social activity – mostly they gather to recite religious texts – Hindu, Islamic or Christian – but there are also a group or two playing carrom or antakshari. Some younger prisoners do vigorous exercises, particularly the Latin American prisoners mostly here for drug offences. An earlier, much-loved Lady Superintendent had begun colouring activities with pencils on printed designs, for which the prisoners also earned some pocket money, but ever since a girl tried to cut her wrist with the blade of a sharpener it has been stopped. Sleeping, gossiping and crying are the favourite pastimes, but fighting is not far behind. There are fights in every queue, and there are queues for everything – getting canteen, using the toilet, OPD with the Jail Doctor, collecting bhatta ...

But yes, unlike in the Phansi Yard, here we have TV, usually playing saas–bahu and naagin serials, true to its idiot-box nomenclature; with the remote firmly in the hands of the kaamwalis (these are older undertrials who are paid safai karmis [sanitation workers], but basically play the role of Warders and enforce discipline, including by slapping and [wo]manhandling other prisoners!). It is only with great social adroitness that one manages to see NDTV for maybe five minutes – 'just the headlines, please' – at teatime.

Watching TV after a long time does give one a sense of normality. It is also a barometer of the jail. Serials and reality shows are all forgotten when Aryan Khan is arrested. The entire period that he is in jail, and for all the hours that the TV is permitted to be on, the only channels being followed are the news channels reporting the case. The women are gathered around waiting with bated breath and largely in great sympathy with the young man. 'Poor boy' ... 'And no possession either!' 'It's vindictiveness!' There are long discussions on the possibilities of bail. Contrary to the superficial understanding that prisoners are 'not aware of their rights', I find that actually many of them soon learn from the more 'professional' among them, like prisoners under PITA or NDPS. The problem is not so much lack of knowledge on their part as their actually getting proper legal representation.

When Covid comes, it's a nightmare. The day after the Prime Minister's announcement of the first lockdown, the prisoners go berserk, refusing breakfast and lunch. They gather in the compound, climb on the compound walls banging thalis and shouting 'Let us go, let us go!! Let us go and die with our families!' It is only after the Superintendent comes in and addresses the courtyard full of anxious undertrials, listens to some of the more vocal ones and gets the suo motu order of the Supreme Court read out – the order says prisoners accused of crimes carrying a sentence of seven years or less will be considered for interim bail – that the prisoners calm down, line up for the evening bhatta and return to their barracks. The next day, all pickles and masala powders anyone has purchased from the Canteen are confiscated – as a precaution against a jail riot. The 'ringleaders' of the earlier day's demonstrations – mostly younger and looser-tongued prisoners staying in the first-floor barracks – are transferred to another Circle where the women with children are housed. They have been identified by the kaamwalis. Then one day we all officially bang thalis, as directed by the Prime Minister, under the supervision of the Lady Jailer.

The first wave of Covid is relatively gentle on Byculla Jail. There is only one detected case. Of course, all mulakats and court visits have stopped. There are no letters and no newspapers. It is as if a pause button has been pressed on life. For the period of a month, even the Women Constables are forced to stay in jail fifteen days at a time – the jail has been 'sealed'. The prisoners snicker gleefully when the Constables grumble incessantly about this. Surprisingly, the inflow of prisoners does not cease. Some of them are in for violations of Covid regulations and there are even several middle-class ones accused of Covid-related crimes like faking vaccination certificates or illegal sale of Remdesivir. The connection to the outside world is only through the screaming of the news channels, and we watch with a sense of disbelief as anchors blame the Tablighi Jamaat for spreading Covid and crores of migrants begin walking home . . .

I am very pleasantly surprised to see two very sincere Lady Jailers go from barrack to barrack after bandi on several evenings, trying to fill in forms for interim bail, albeit mechanically. But the judicial system fails us. The guidelines of the 'high-powered committee' constituted in Maharashtra to supervise the grant of Covid bail are so full of ifs and buts that a mere handful of petty thieves are released, some of them only to return.

The second wave is unadulterated misery. In my own barrack, then housing around fifty-six prisoners, some seventeen have tested positive, including those sleeping on either side of me. The positives among women prisoners, totalling nearly sixty in number across barracks, are separated, asked to pack a bag and told that they will be taken elsewhere. Some are crying out of uncertainty, but later it turns out that they are being taken to a Covid-care centre of the Municipal Corporation where they get a bed(!) and a mattress(!!) and tasty vegetarian food provided by an NGO(!!!) and are monitored by doctors on a daily basis. They return quite happy and full of stories, and keep trying to be taken back there again. Meanwhile, people like me, who have not tested positive but are running a fever, are all crammed into the worst barrack – Barrack No. 6 upstairs, and locked in completely. No time allowed outside in the corridor or compound, or even to meet our friends among the inmates who sometimes sneak their way there to commiserate through the bars.

The forty-five days I spent in that 'quarantine barrack' I shall never forget. I had an extremely weakening diarrhoea for about a month. Everyone was sick and no kaamwali was allowed in the barrack. Three out of the four toilets there were choked and no one had the energy to keep the barrack clean. Even food had to be collected through the bars or from just outside the barrack. By that time, thanks to a PUCL petition in the Bombay High Court, weekly phone calls of ten minutes to family members had started in jail, but not for us of the quarantine barrack. The ridiculous part was that the new admissions were brought there too, thus exposing us and them to Covid infection all over again. On occasion, the number of occupants of the 'quarantine barrack' would even go up to seventy. And each time my two weeks of isolation would end, I would be sent to hospital, perhaps only to collect a report, and since I had been there I would again go into quarantine for another two weeks. When I was finally released from Barrack No. 6 to return downstairs to Barrack No. 2, that really felt like bail! Also, Shoma Di and I were together again, both housed in a barrack for over-forty-fives, who were the first group to be vaccinated.

Later, I discussed the irrationality of the quarantining procedure in jail with the jail doctors, and they agreed candidly. They were just following the regulations and notifications handed down to them. It was the jail administration and not the doctors that took the decisions. Clearly, an overcrowded jail is not the place to deal with an epidemic. The first priority should have been decongestion – sending as many people as possible home. The tragedy was, the one prisoner who died – an elderly woman of the scheduled caste Mang community, already suffering from hypertension and arthritis – had been granted bail many months earlier, but like many other poor people in jail had simply not been able to arrange the sureties.

One of the things I learnt in Byculla was about the creativity of the prisoners even under such difficult circumstances. They would go to great lengths to get notebooks, crayons and felt pens to diligently illustrate their weekly letters to children, spouses and lovers (no doubt the Constables had a whale of a time reading those!). Then there were all the greeting cards – for birthdays, New Year, Diwali, Eid, Friendship Day, Valentine's Day, Ganpati festival . . . and just for nothing at all. Shoma Di was in great demand for her beautiful sketches. And also for teaching English. The enthusiasm with which young prisoners began attending basic literacy, numeracy and English classes organized by my co-accused Jyoti Jagtap was remarkable. Unfortunately, they were nipped in the bud by Covid. Needles were prohibited, but everyone knew that some amount of stitching was necessary just to keep the few clothes prisoners possessed in repair, so a blind eye was turned. Some prisoners were expert seamstresses, using threads from the old ghongris, chaddars and old clothes, and earned enough 'Canteen' through mending work. And there was an amazing Latin American prisoner who was truly a designer – the bags she could conjure up out of worn nighties, the little pouches she could make from dupattas, the tops she could make from old kurtas, adding frills, laces, and pockets from old jeans . . . they would have put professional designers to shame!

I have already talked about the jail recipes devised at Yerawada to make food edible. In Byculla, where I celebrated my sixtieth birthday, my fellow prisoners took resourcefulness to a new level. A group of youngsters led by Jyoti made me a cake. They kneaded Marie biscuits into a base, covered it with Britannia rusks soaked in sugar solution, and iced it with Bournvita paste. It was decorated with my name in jam! I don't think I've ever had such a tasty or beautiful birthday cake, and the whole barrack wanted a piece! It was a wonderful excuse to gather, sing and yes, Aunty was forced to dance – pretty clumsily, I admit.

But for me, the most important thing about my time in Byculla was that I became the in-house Vakeel Aunty. Once the prisoners realized that I was not judgemental about them, that I kept their confidence and would not gossip, there was a great demand for me to read their chargesheets and orders, and to advise them about their lawyers and legal strategies. It was only with trust that those chargesheets, carefully hidden away in jholas – usually unread, for most women were illiterate – finally saw the light of day. Those who had families tended to send them away unread, and some of them now asked for them to be sent back. It was in Byculla that I really understood the absolute inadequacy of legal aid and its absence of accountability to the prisoner. I have spoken elsewhere in this book about my suggestions for its improvement. I am happy that finally, during the tenure of CJI U.U. Lalit, the system of District Legal Aid Defence Counsel of the National Legal Services Authority has begun to be implemented in many districts across the country, thus providing enthusiastic young lawyers with a chance to exclusively devote themselves to legal aid with a reasonable remuneration. It's a small step in the right direction, but not nearly enough.

During Covid, I must have written hundreds of

applications on behalf of prisoners, all in duplicate and by hand in Hindi (since whatever I had learnt of Marathi was still not good enough). There were all sorts of pleas: for video mulakats with male family members lodged in other jails; to get copies of chargesheets; for default bail, medical bail and interim bail; to get jail transfers; to be allowed phone calls with lawyers; to be taken to hospital. I wrote to courts, to jail authorities, to the Chief Medical Officer, to lawyers, and on occasion even to the High Court Registry. (The only applications I refused to write were complaints of prisoners against one another.) I would sit up late at night – under the bright tube lights – doing this; and sometimes the Constables on their late Night Rounds would tell me good-naturedly to go to sleep. I wrote countless applications for interim Covid bail – for women above seventy-five; women with TB, AIDS, brain tumour and cancer; pregnant women; women with infants; and women with comorbidities like hypertension and diabetes. In fact, after a time, the Lady Jailer would send me prisoners needing applications to be written. Having said that, my failure rate was spectacular – not a single application for Covid bail succeeded, though in my opinion they all stood a very good chance. Even in other cases, my successes were few enough to count – getting a copy of her chargesheet for one frustrated young prisoner; uniting a Pardhi prisoner with her one-year-old who was alone 'outside' with neighbours; filing a default bail application for a vocal young woman trapped in a first-time drug offence; getting a few prisoners their court appearances or legal aid lawyers and – with the help of my lawyers – getting bail for an intellectually disabled beggar woman accused of murdering her husband. This tedious and unrewarding process made me acutely aware of the enormity of the task before the legal system if it really intends that prisoners be properly represented and get a fair and speedy trial. Any pride I might have had in my lawyerly skills was completely humbled.

My becoming a de facto unofficial lawyer for many prisoners after I entered Byculla was what brought my diary-writing to a halt. If anything, the sketches of the prisoners in Byculla might have been even more interesting, and now I had much more time and opportunity to speak to them too. But since I was representing them, it would not have been ethical for me to betray their trust. Also, I was far too busy. Now my notebooks were full of cryptic pointers for the applications I was to elaborate on their behalf – undertrial number (UT No.), crime number, police station, court name, Sections of Acts, dates, family histories, the prisoner's own defence, description of her illnesses and what not. They were not just 'applications', but lives.

On 1 December 2021, several months after the judgment had been reserved for orders, the Bombay High Court granted me bail. My heart was torn in two because Shoma Di and my other co-accused did not get relief. The sessions court laid down the conditions of my bail on 8 December – it confined me to the jurisdiction of the NIA Court at Mumbai and directed fortnightly reporting at the local police station. I must say that I have been extremely lucky to have received warm and generous support and solidarity from friends, lawyers, unions and the social activists of Mumbai in my 'rehabilitation'.

Today I live, exiled from my beloved Chhattisgarh, in a suburb of Mumbai, mostly alone except when my daughter visits me. I do legal work for unions for my living. Yet, more than a year after my release on bail, the lives of women prisoners continue to haunt me. I dream of them, worry about them and wonder what became of them. On those rare days when I get a phone call from an unknown number – 'Hey Aunty, remember me? I got released!' – I feel a lightness that I can't explain. And I know these feelings are going to be with me as long as I live.

Jail Glossary

302: Section 302 of the Indian Penal Code is for murder. Prisoners accused of murder are one of the categories specifically counted each day. In Maharashtra, murder undertrials wear green saris (which are generally worn only by convicts) though this practice does not seem to have legal sanction.

BC: The name for the kitchen in a jail, though what the initials stand for nobody seems to remember. In the Yerawada Women's Jail, the BC was run by 12 or 13 women, mostly convicts, who were sent to work early in the morning by 5.30 a.m. and worked on and off throughout the day till about 5.30 p.m. to prepare food for 300–350 prisoners in the jail.

Bageechewali: Prisoner who works in the garden for a meagre pay.

Bai: All the Constables are referred to as Bai by prisoners in Yerawada. In Byculla, which is an urban undertrial prison with a lot more non-Maharashtrian occupants, usually Constables are referred to as Madam.

Bakery: The Main Jail at Yerawada is famous for its bakery items, which are prepared by male prisoners. For Christmas, prisoners are allowed to purchase cakes and cupcakes from the bakery from their PPC (see below) accounts.

Bandi: Bandi means the process of locking in. Prisoners are locked in from about 5.30 p.m. to 7 a.m., and again between 12 noon and 3 p.m.

Barrack: Barracks are the long halls in which prisoners sleep and keep their belongings. In Yerawada there are only rudimentary toilet facilities attached to a barrack (one toilet and one bathroom), and one is meant to bathe or relieve oneself outside the barrack in the daytime.

Bhatta: The word literally means 'allowance' and comes from the fact that the jail manual prescribes certain quantities of food by weight to be provided to prisoners. Bhatta includes breakfast served at 7 a.m., lunch at 11 a.m., tea at 3 p.m. and dinner at 4.30 p.m. Also see the section on Food.

Canteen: This is a sort of shop on the premises of the jail from where a prisoner can purchase items from a limited and sometimes scarce array of soaps, shampoos, oils and creams; snacks, pickles and powders; stationery and pens; sanitary napkins and diapers; but not at will. Usually, prisoners will be allowed to go there once in fifteen days or once a month, barrack by barrack.

Cell: In the Yerawada Women's Jail, the only individual cells (four in all) are in the Phansi Yard, now known as Separate

Yard. I was lodged in one of them. The cell was about ten (of my) paces long and four paces wide. It had bars in the front and an Indian-style toilet at the back.

Chaddar: A rough white bed sheet given as part of a prisoner's bedding.

Children: Women prisoners can keep their children up to six years of age with them. Then they have to be handed over to a relative outside or sent to a children's home. Between the ages of four and six they are sent to a playschool located just outside the Gate of the jail. Children are given a special diet in the jail and are attended to by paediatricians who visit weekly.

Diet: Prisoners of very low weight or suffering from malnutrition, or from ailments like TB, HIV, cancer, etc., are given a special diet at Yerawada, including two eggs a day, 250 ml of milk and a fixed number of pavs. This is usually decided by a Diet Committee, which sits every three to six months. The Jail Doctor can also prescribe boiled diets, saltless diets, etc., temporarily for prisoners.

Factory: The Factory in Yerawada is a large shed with a tin roof divided into three parts – one for rolling out agarbattis, one for sewing and weaving work, and the Spark Minda shed where small auto parts are manufactured.

Gandhi Yard: One of the yards in the Yerawada Main Jail. Gandhiji spent long periods in Yerawada. In fact, negotiations with Dr Ambedkar resulting in the Poona Pact took place there.

Gate: This is the lobby-like place between the outer fortress-like walls and the inner iron gates to the Compounds. It has the office of the Jailer Madam on one side and on the other the room in which the strip-search takes place. A Constable sits at the Gate checking persons entering and leaving through a smaller door in the large iron gate. On court dates, police Guards come and wait outside with warrants to take particular prisoners to court, and there is a meticulous system of entering their names, their court details and the accompanying Guards' names in a register.

Ghongri: A rough woven blanket, rather prickly to the touch.

Godaam: A godown or place of storage. In Yerawada there was one godaam in each Compound. In our Convict Compound, the godaam was in the Hospital Barrack. It stored long and short brooms, bundles of green saris, blouses and petticoats, the extra clothes of the prisoners, spare utensils, spare bedding, old registers. Prisoners are not allowed to keep many possessions with them. So, for instance, all our spare books would also have to be stored there.

Goliwale: Psychiatric patients are referred to as '*goliwale*', which is a tad kinder than 'mental', which is the term prisoners normally use for the mentally challenged. A psychiatrist comes once a week, but usually only to treat those who cannot be 'managed' by the Warders; there is little notion of otherwise normal prisoners getting therapy.

Green sari: The uniform of convicts is a green sari, white petticoat and white blouse – all of cotton. But among the undertrials, only those accused of murder wear a green sari.

Guard: The Maharashtra State Police (Guards) are a different cadre from the Maharashtra Prison Police and come to escort prisoners to and from the court.

Hauz: The large water tank in the common bathrooms in both Compounds. Each common bathroom is a long, enclosed space with a hauz and a drain running down its length. Most of the women bathe here, but there are a few bathing cubicles on both sides of the drain with waist-high doors where one can take a bucket inside and have a more private bath. These are generally used by older women.

Jhadti: All searches are referred to as jhadti, but actually there are different kinds:

- Body-strip search, which is carried out every time a prisoner leaves or enters jail, whether for court, or hospital or on a jail transfer.

- Search of the barracks. For this, all the prisoners line up outside and the Constables enter the barrack and just empty out all their belongings on the floor and search for prohibited articles like needles, nailcutters, steel clips, fermented articles, extra sets of clothes, etc.

Kaamwali: This term was used more in Byculla Jail than at Yerawada Jail and refers to a prisoner who is a modestly paid sanitary worker. Kaamwalis do a lot of clerical and managerial work, and also have a disciplinary role as they generally act as Warders in the Byculla barracks.

Karanti: This is a colloquialization of the word 'quarantine', it appears. The Phansi Yard or Separate Yard is also referred to as Karanti. We were quite nervous, thinking it had something to do with (electric) current.

Kundewali: This term was used only in Yerawada Jail and dates back to a time when prisoners working as paid sanitary workers would remove kundas (earthen pots) of excreta from the barracks. There are no dry latrines in Yerawada Jail now.

Likhaan: Every convicted prisoner has a record in which a calculation is made of all the days spent in jail as an undertrial in all the cases she is accused in, those being deductible from the respective sentences; the days spent as a convict; additional days that may be in lieu of not paying a fine; and finally a calculation of how many days' remission has been granted for work performed or for good conduct or talent exhibited. When a prisoner is due to be released, her likhaan will first arrive at the jail.

Lock-up: There are two kinds of lock-ups (both equally dirty):

- The police lock-up attached to the police station in which the FIR of an accused has been lodged. A person here is in PC or police custody (as opposed to being in JC or judicial custody, when they are sent to jail). The police apply to the court for this custody in order to carry out interrogation.

- The court lock-up is situated on the premises of a court. Prisoners are brought here from jail and wait there to be called by the respective courts which are trying them.

MC: This is the term used for menstrual cycle. The Women's jail maintains a register to record the menstrual cycles of all the women. And also of their utilization of sanitary napkins.

Madam: In Yerawada Jail, only the Jailer or Assistant Jailer with their 'brown belts' are called Madam. The Constables, including the Head Constables (all wearing 'black belts') are called Bai.

Minda: The company is actually Spark Minda, but in jail it is referred to as Minda. The work of the company is carried out in a part of the Factory and is supervised by one or two company officials. In the Yerawada Women's Jail, twenty-five to thirty prisoners used to carry out the manufacture of automotive locksets for the company between 8 a.m. and 4 p.m. from Monday to Saturday.

Moka (MCOCA): The Maharashtra Control of Organised Crime Act is a stringent act, basically promulgated to deal with the proliferation of gang wars and extortions that plagued Mumbai in the eighties and nineties. It has draconian provisions, such as admissibility of a confession made to a policeman, stringent conditions of bail, a possibility of extension for the time period in which to file a chargesheet, etc.

Mulakat: Women prisoners have two kinds of mulakats (visits):

- With visitors from 'outside', including relatives, friends and lawyers, though at the discretion of the jail. They can see the visitors through a glass pane and speak to them through a phone.

- With male family members lodged in the Main Jail, for which women prisoners and their children are ferried across the road in jail vans. They meet with their male family members as visitors do – see them through a glass pane and speak to them through a phone.

NDPS: The Narcotic Drugs and Psychotropic Substances Act, 1985 – a stringent act dealing with offences relating to cultivation, possession, sale, transportation, export and trafficking of drugs.

Open: A short form for Open Jail; but in Yerawada Jail, it refers to the rice and vegetable fields of the jail adjoining the residential campuses. Female and male convicts go there to carry out farming work, for which they receive payment as well as a remission in their sentence. The produce of the Open fields is consumed in the jail and also sold to earn revenue for the jail.

POCSO: The Protection of Children from Sexual Offences Act, 2012, prescribes stringent punishment for sexual harassment, sexual assault or pornography relating to children, creates special courts to try such offences and special procedures to be followed.

PPC: Prisoners' Personal Cash. A relative or friend of a prisoner can send her money, which is put into her PPC. When I came to Byculla, the maximum amount was increased to Rs 4,500 per month. This can be used to buy items from the Canteen or 'special' items (see below).

Patti: A narrow strip of dhurrie on which a prisoner sleeps. About 6 feet long and 18 inches wide. These are woven in the Main Jail.

Phansi Yard: This means death row. Phansi literally means hanging. It is the Phansi Yard where I and my co-accused Professor Shoma Sen were lodged. Two death-row prisoners were our neighbours.

PITA: The Immoral Traffic (Prevention) Act, 1956, which criminalizes sex work by making ownership or management of a brothel and soliciting for customers illegal. It also provides for rehabilitation of trafficked women.

Round: Every week on Saturday in Yerawada there is a Big Round – which means that the Superintendent and a retinue of officers, including the Jailer of the Women's Jail, the Canteen-in-Charge, the Jail Doctor, Social Worker, Teacher, etc., go round the barracks in turn. All prisoners line up outside their barrack and can make written or oral requests. Mid-week, the Lady Jailer of the Women's Jail conducts a smaller Round with Senior Constables.

Sometimes there are Rounds made by the District Judge, the Inspector General of Prisons and the Director General, Prisons, and even the Human Rights Commission. But prisoners are not encouraged to express their grievances and are sometimes actively discouraged from doing so by the jail authorities.

Sanstha: The word means 'institution', but in a jail context it usually refers to:

- a children's home where the children of women prisoners are sent after they reach the age of six and where they will remain until they become adults, unless a family member applies to and is permitted to take them home

and sometimes to:

- an NGO which carries out activities in the jail.

Senior: A Head Constable is referred to as a Senior. She is distinguished from other Constables by the yellow stripes on her shoulder straps.

Separate Yard: The modern name for the Phansi Yard is Separate Yard.

Shiksha Vibhag: The Marathi term for Convict Compound (a literal translation of vibhag would be department).

Showroom: Yerawada Jail has a Showroom where articles crafted by prisoners are exhibited and also sold. The Showroom displays bed covers, towels, blankets, rugs and mats; Paithani saris, pants, shirts and bags; Kolhapuri chappals and shoes; stools, chairs, tables, sofas, dressing tables and small wooden temples; and bakery items like breads, biscuits and nankhatais.

Solar: The Yerawada Women's Jail uses a solar heater to heat water. Infants and children and the elderly among the prisoners generally have priority in accessing this limited supply.

Special: These are treats available to a prisoner who can purchase them from their PPC accounts (see above).

Tai: A Warder who is a long-standing convicted prisoner chosen to manage, supervise and discipline a barrack is also known as a Tai, which literally means elder sister in Marathi. They are given yellow saris to wear.

Toll: A gong hanging near the Gate which is sounded at every opening and closing, and also at the beginning and end of the afternoon bandi.

Total: Every morning and evening prisoners are counted. In the morning there is just a total count, and in the evening they are also counted according to category of offence, though the Jail Manual does not specify any such categorization. In Byculla the categorization was 'MCOCA, NDPS, Section 302 (murder accused), Maovaadi (Maoist), Naxal, Bangladeshi undertrials, Bangladeshi convicts, and 'Itar' (all the rest).

Tower: These are towers in the Yerawada Main Jail, on the top of which Constables are placed on duty to get a bird's-eye view of the entire jail. Both men and women Constables are given this duty.

UAPA: The stringent Unlawful Activities (Prevention) Act, 1967, which bans certain 'unlawful associations' and 'terrorist organisations' and punishes activities connected thereto. Prisoners under UAPA have greater restriction on their visitors – only blood relatives and lawyers are permitted.

Undertrial Compound: The other Compound of the jail which housed most of the undertrials. It contained two barracks, toilets, a Bath-House and an Office building containing a Library.

UT Card: This is the card given to an undertrial prisoner when she enters the jail. It contains her name as written in the FIR, the crime number (or FIR number), the name of the police station and the Sections of the Indian Penal Code or other Acts under which she is accused. Subsequently, it is supposed to also record the dates of her court hearings, but is rarely properly updated.

Yellow Sari: A Warder (see below) gets to wear a yellow sari to distinguish her from the ordinary convicts who wear green saris.

Warder: A convicted prisoner who is in charge of the discipline of a barrack. She is supposed to stay awake for part of the night, usually from 12 midnight to 3 a.m., to keep a watch on other prisoners in the barrack.

Watchman: Prisoner, usually a convict, in charge of a part of the Factory.

Zamanatdar: Person who stands surety for an accused to be released on bail.

Acknowledgements

This book came to be because of the amazing resilience of women prisoners whom I lived with, not only the ones in Yerawada whom I write about, but also those in Byculla whom I thought it was better to represent as their lawyer. Professor Shoma Sen, my neighbour in the Phansi Yard, was the first to read my scribbles and encourage me. To them I owe my greatest debt.

After I was released on bail in December 2021, I typed the notes out and circulated them to a few friends; it seemed to be the best way I could share my experiences, otherwise difficult to talk about. Many thanks to Uma, Sharmila, Rakhi, Smita and Lara, who urged me to publish these as a book. And most of all to senior journalist Ajaz Ashraf who I came to know over an interview, and who actually pushed me to take the first steps.

I am grateful to Chiki Sarkar, who with her characteristic boldness and sensitivity took up this project for publication with enthusiasm. It was Anjali Puri who worked hard to get under the skin of the book, and patiently dealt with my occasional stubbornness, to bring the rough manuscript into its present shape. Thanks to Arani, Devangana and the entire editing team who carried out the finishing touches.

If this book can interest the reader enough to pause and think a little about the world behind bars, it will have served its purpose.